In The Silence

A 90 Day Devotional for Women

Tina McCay

All Scripture is taken from the King James Bible.

Contents

Week 1

*Fit for
the Masters Use*

Do You Smell Like a Christian?

For we are labourers together with God: ye are God's husbandry, ye are God's building.

(I Corinthians 3:9)

I remember as a child, my dad would come home from work and immediately hop in the shower. We knew that he would visit us afterwards, but we had to let him shower first. He was a transmission specialist, and between the fluids and greases, combined with his sweat, he stank!

Well, what brought this to memory was a personal time when we had a work party at the church. It was hot out, and we were doing some rather hard yard work, painting and gardening. Some ladies volunteered to fix a meal for us all to enjoy after we were finished. But when we came in to sit with them at the table, they let us know that we didn't smell very pleasant. I was a bit taken aback by the comment. I didn't smell bad to myself. I leaned over and sniffed the person next to me, who also sniffed in my direction. We didn't notice anything to complain about. We washed up and enjoyed our meal together. Yet, throughout the meal, the topic of how badly we smelled kept coming up. Then the thought hit me. Those of us who were working outside all smelled the same! We wore the aroma of the yard, the machines, the dirt and paint we were using. But the ladies inside smelled of food. Hmm. Christ has given us a job to do. He said that he wants us to work in his field and that the harvest is ready. He's out there working and has a job for each of us to do individually. Sometimes my only job is to entertain the little ones. But it's a place to fill. So, when the harvest is over, and He calls us in to sit with him around the supper table, what will we smell like to him?

Takeaway: I want to smell like I spent my life working alongside of Christ. Lord, help me be faithful to your work.

Say What?

If a man therefore purge himself from these, he shall be a vessel unto honour, sanctified, and meet for the master's use, and prepared unto every good work. (II Timothy 2:21)

I started a new mail route. It goes through the heart of the Native American reservation and an area filled with drug use. After a few days on the route, I experienced a very stoned man who was yelling atrocities at me and demanding that I tell him where Karl was. I prayed a quick breath of a prayer and answered him with all the strength I had. "I'm sorry, I don't know who that is."

He began to call me all sorts of unfavorable names to which I stated, "That is not my name." Then I drove away to the next set of mailboxes.

He ran after me, and the scene began again and again and again. Finally, he said, "Do you have a name?" I replied, "Yes, and maybe someday when you can talk with respect, I will tell it to you," then I drove away at top speed to get away.

About two weeks later, he was standing behind his mailbox waiting for me. I again breathed a quick prayer and said, "Hello."

He was sober this time and said, "Hello, my name is William. What is your name?" Truthfully, I didn't want to tell him, but he was being respectful. So, I told him, "My name is Tina." He smiled and said, "It's nice to meet you, Tina".

Over the next few years, William and I would have many encounters that ended with me driving away abruptly because he was stoned and rude. One fateful day, I had already had a struggle with other stoned individuals and was stopping at the local grocery store for a quick item to fix for supper. I was just starting my car and looked up to see William and his woman (what he calls her, I do not know her name) running in my direction. OH NO!!! Lord, I did not have the strength for another encounter today! So, I pretended to not see them and put my car in reverse. Only, I put it into drive by mistake and drove right into the concrete light pole in front of me. Ugh! The transmission hose was torn free from the bottom of the radiator and fluid was quirting all over the parking lot and William was still coming towards me!

He said, "You shouldn't be in such a hurry all the time. I've been trying to talk to you." I said, "Yes, I know. Sorry, but I was trying to avoid you. I've already had a hard day." He hung his head and said, "Oh, I get it." To which I apologized. He looked at my car and said, "I can fix this if you have a knife." My first thought was, ARE YOU CRAZY? I DON'T WANT TO GIVE A DRUG ADDICT A KNIFE! But instead, I said, "Sure, I have one in my lunch bag." So, during the next few moments, William and I sat on the ground together and fixed my car as he told me how the two of them had been in treatment for the last year. They had been searching for me to say thank you. He further stated that because of me, he realized that he didn't like himself very much. I felt awful and said I was sorry for being so rude to him. I knew I could be nicer. But he told me that he needed that from me. That he wanted to be like me. He wanted to be someone that people respect. To be someone that HE respects. I just sat there softly crying and told him, "Thank you for sharing that with me".

I've seen them many times since then and have always had the pleasure of saying, "Hi, it's good to see you today."

Takeaway: God wants me to be faithful to Him. I may not know how He's using me to reach others. Thank you, Lord, for using me and allowing me to be a vessel of honor for you.

Win the Race

L *et us run with patience the race that is set before us, looking unto Jesus the author and finisher of our faith; who for the joy that was set before him endured the cross, despising the shame, and is set down at the right hand of the throne of God. (Hebrews 12; 1-2)*

If you would, imagine for a moment that you are a NASCAR racer. The expense of such racing is so high that you require a sponsor to fund your endeavor. Furthermore, you need a certain amount of skill before a sponsor will even consider your need for money.

The Apostle Paul compared our lives to a race. Notice how he said to look unto Jesus, the author and finisher of our faith. He's the sponsor of the race that you call your life. Like any sponsor, he has rules to abide by. An earthly sponsor requires you to wear his logo on your helmet, clothing, safety gear, racecar, water bottles, thermoses, anything identified with you as a racer, including on the uniforms of your crew and any advertisements. We are to do the same for Christ. *(1 Corinthians 10;31) Whether therefore ye eat, or drink, or whatsoever ye do, do all to the glory of God.* If you are a child of God, you are to be identified as sponsored by Christ.

A good sponsor will give you a budget large enough to supply everything needed to win the race and bring honor and glory to the company's name. Like

Pennzoil who has sponsored racers for years and become a household name. They supply the car, safety equipment, training, crew, etc. Christ isn't limited by earthly wealth. He has all the resources of heaven to call on for your needs. He gave everything to save you (sponsor you) in the race of life. The prize being your faith revealed in glory. Can you picture it? You and I, standing together in the winner's circle with Christ.

How are we going to win this race? First, we need a vehicle. Consider yourself as your race car. You are composed of body, soul, and spirit. Like a car composed of body, engine, and drivetrain.

You must be able to control the car to keep the body intact. If the body is destroyed, the engine and drive train are rendered useless. Who has ever seen an engine or transmission ripping up the racetrack without a chassis connected? In comparison, we must keep our fleshly bodies intact or healthy. We must also keep ourselves as best we can from sin so we can finish this race with honor. Finally, we must also show up for the race. Christ wants us to reach the world with the gospel. How that looks in your life is individual to you. Maybe you could give to missions, or you just pass out smiles as you do your errands. Get creative. But get busy for Christ.

Takeaway: My race with Christ involves more than mere church attendance, though that is very important. I should be at it every day if I want to stand in the winner's circle. Lord, help me to see what you would like me to do each day in honor of you.

Chameleons

A *nd be not conformed to this world: but be ye transformed by the renewing of your mind, that ye may prove what is that good, and acceptable, and perfect, will of God. (Romans 12:2)*

To the weak became I as weak, that I might gain the weak: I am made all things to all men, that I might by all means save some. (I Corinthians 9:22)

Have you ever heard people say that the Bible was contradictory? The two verses listed above would suggest that to be true unless you really take into consideration what they're saying.

For example, chameleons are amazing little creatures. They have the ability to adapt to their surroundings and become somewhat invisible.

Now take into thought the two verses listed above. In the first verse, Romans 12:2, Christians are told to avoid conforming to the world in such a way that the Savior becomes invisible to those around us. As many preachers have taught, if we live like the world, why would they want to change to live in our beliefs? After all, we are no different from them. The other truth of this is that if we indulge in worldly practices, we will lose our testimony and seem like one who mocks in a moment of witnessing.

Yet in, I Corinthians 9:22, Christians are charged to adapt to the cultures and needs of the world in order to let Christ be known by those around us. If we are so segregated from our neighbors, how can we witness to them? We must have an avenue to reach them. So, as the Apostle Paul states here, he identifies with people in such a way as to not offend them. He won't present himself as being above them. However, he will not defame the character of Christ in the process.

So, back to the thought, how can we fulfill both? We must become like those chameleons. They have the ability to transition into their surroundings, yet they do not become the item that they emulate. They fluidly take on the image of their surroundings while still remaining their own individual. So, Christians must live in this world but maintain their own identity in Christ. Simply put, we have to live in this world, but the world doesn't have to live in us. Christ lives there.

Takeaway: Let your witness shine so brightly that others see and desire to know the source. But protect it with all diligence by keeping a needed separation. Lord, I pray that the ladies reading this know how very precious they are in your eyes and that their testimony is their greatest asset for your work.

Safety Talk

Be sober, be vigilant; because your adversary the devil, as a roaring lion, walketh about, seeking whom he may devour: (I Peter 5:8)

Every time you take a commercial air flight, you must go through a preflight safety talk. I remember the first time I heard one. I found myself discreetly searching for a way to turn my seat into a flotation device.

I had the privilege of flying with two of my grandchildren on their first flight, and I watched them as they paid extremely close attention to their first safety demonstration. During the flight, every sound and every adjustment the plane made frightened them and had their full attention. It made me chuckle as I remembered myself all those years ago. It also caused me to think. As a new Christian, I would sit on the edge of my seat and listen intently to every word the preacher had to share from the Bible. I was so very eager to learn more and more. But over time, I began to recognize and expect the messages I would hear at each service. I became comfortable. I should never become so comfortable in my Christian journey that I forget there is an ever-present danger. Satan is like a roaring lion, roaming about, seeking whom he may devour. And, just like the preflight safety talk, I should keep God's word and messages fresh in my heart and mind. So that, in the event of an emergency, I have all the tools necessary for my faith to step into action. I want my faith to be in full force, so it will see me through to safety. PS: I'm still trying to figure out that flotation device.

Takeaway: I need to keep my heart and mind focused so Satan cannot catch me off guard. Lord, help me to study your word and to glean from the preaching of it in church. May my desire to learn of you continue for my entire life.

Reflection Day

This week, we have looked at several verses on making ourselves fit for the service of our Lord. I pray you will spend a few minutes reflecting on how the Lord has used events of this week to speak to you. Here are a few ideas:

How has God spoken to you this week?

In what way did you allow God to use you this week?

How did you reach out to a new person this week?

The Lord's Day

*B*ehold, how good and how pleasant it is for brethren to dwell together in unity!

(Psalm 133:1)

Today is a day set aside for God and family. It is a well-known fact that Sundays are extremely crazy and busy in most households. Please take your family to church and enjoy your day with them.

Lord, I pray you will bless and protect this person and their family as they try to honor you with this day. Help them to glean from your word and allow your people to feed their spirit and leave them feeling blessed. Lord, I pray that you will touch this precious person in a way that will open their heart to see you clearly and know how very much they are loved.

Week 2

Being Available for God

Don't Turn Away

A *nd he said unto me, My grace is sufficient for thee: for my strength is made perfect in weakness. Most gladly therefore will I rather glory in my infirmities, that the power of Christ may rest upon me.(II Corinthians 12:9)*

Have you ever encountered a person with special needs while you're in public? Ever caught yourself staring at them without even realizing that you're staring at them? When my son was about five years old, we were at Dairy Queen and saw a lady with no arms. Her hands literally were popping out of her shoulders. And they weren't even full hands. It was an interesting sight to see.

She ordered an ice cream cone, and I didn't realize that I was staring and so was my little one. She looked at us and asked, "Can I help you?" I was at a loss for words and my son pops out, "Can I watch you eat that ice cream cone?" His voice sounded so excited! And she looked at me as I smiled back at her and told her, "You are amazing! Would you want to share a table with us?" She smiled and agreed.

She sat at the table and sanitized her foot and rinsed it with a wet paper towel then grabbed her ice cream cone out of the cup holder and began to eat it with her toes like it was nothing to her! Of course, she's been doing this all her life. My son pops his feet up on the table and says, "Me! Me!!" I had to tell him that he would have to try that at home. She started laughing and we had a great time together for about thirty minutes, just sharing ice cream and chitchat. May I say, we all have flaws. We all have weaknesses. We all have little deformities. Why not turn them into a strength as this beautiful woman did? What a testimony she had! And forever, my son and I have the memory of that half an hour that she spent with us at Dairy Queen. Let your weaknesses define you in such a way that you leave a positive impact on others. God gave them to you for a very special reason. So, use them for His glory.

Takeaway: I pray that you can use me, Lord, even in my weakest points.

The Clouds

The LORD is slow to anger, and great in power, and will not at all acquit the wicked: the LORD hath his way in the whirlwind and in the storm, and the clouds are the dust of his feet. (Nahum 1:3)

We had a dear old lady in our church named Miss Dolly. She was a wonderful example of faithfulness. She was in church every time the doors were open. She gave to anyone in need and her doors were always open to a traveling preacher or missionary. She read her Bible through every year. Sometimes twice! Anyway, one particular day, she came to church so very excited. She said she had a blessing to share. While reading her Bible that morning, she had discovered something she had never noticed in all her eighty-six years. She asked everyone, "Did you know that the clouds are the dust of God's feet?" The joy on her face as she shared that with us was indescribable. It was a very cloudy day. She had been a widow for a very long time. She'd also lost one of her sons in an accident and she was pretty lonely.

I think that this verse helped her to realize the truth of when God says he is with us always. She further shared that all she had to do was look up and know that he was busy taking care of her because there was the dust he was kicking up. How precious is that? Every time you look up and see clouds, you can know that God is actively pacing back and forth in your area. That he is aware of what's happening right now where you stand. Very rarely is there a day in my area where there's not at least a little puff of a cloud. In fact, the sky is packed with them the whole winter! We rarely see sunlight until spring. So, remember that in the winter of your life. God is really busy taking care of the things that are affecting you. He's really busy taking care of the things that have you down. He never leaves you.

Takeaway: God is in control of everything, and he is actively working in my life. Thank you, Lord, for giving us visual evidence that you are all around us.

Better to Obey

And Samuel said, Hath the Lord as great delight in burnt offerings and sacrifices, as in obeying the voice of the Lord? Behold, to obey is better than sacrifice, and to hearken than the fat of rams. (I Samuel 15:22)

We can learn so many lessons by watching animals. The Bible tells us to consider the ant. Today, I would like to share an example from our farm. Horses are majestic creatures. They are beautiful, graceful, yet they are also very stubborn. The tribe brought us a wild mustang, and we bred her with a beautiful quarter horse. The result was that now we had a very handsome young stallion. We tried to teach him how to do things. However, he would buck and kick us every step of the way. I am a gentle teacher, so I tried to lovingly teach him how to do things. I spent weeks bribing and coaxing him to try new things. But in the end, all that love and kindness bestowed upon him only allowed me to put a halter on him and lead him around. Well, the day came when my husband led him to the round pen and cracked the whip. He was then forced to run in circles...this direction, that direction, faster, slower. He would be allowed to stop at times, and my husband would raise his outstretched hand and call him over. But instead of coming to my husband, he would look for a way of escape. So, the process started again. He would run in circles in this direction, then that direction, until the time came when he finally bowed his head and walked over to my husband's outstretched hand in full submission. When he finally acknowledged my husband as his master, he was able to be taught. See, there's a whole world out there that we wanted to explore with this young stallion. But it wouldn't be good for him or us to do that before he was ready. He had to learn obedience before he could be trusted outside of the round pen. Are you running in circles in your life? Maybe God is trying to tell you to submit to him so he can show you the bigger, better plans he has for you. He's trying to get you ready, are you submitting to his leadership?

Takeaway: Is God the master of your life? Lord, I pray you will help us to submit to your authority in our lives so we can be useful to your plan.

Hugging Porcupines

*I**f it be possible, as much as lieth in you, live peaceably with all men. (Romans 12:18)*

There are people in our lives that will always be against us no matter what. They will always have a negative view towards us no matter how kind we are towards them. This verse in Romans is a strong indicator that God understands that there are times when getting along is a struggle. He also understands that there are people in our lives that make living in peace almost impossible. I was pondering this recently when God gave me a thought. I once had a porcupine in my yard, and I was quite intrigued by it. It had a funny waddle and a cute little face. Sometimes its quills were out and made it look extra fat. At other times, they were drawn in close to where they looked like hair. I wanted to learn more about this untouchable creature, so I fed it, and I watched it. As I did this day to day, it became less leery of me. It seemed to want my attention after a while. But you know what? It was still a one-sided friendship. I still needed to keep myself at a safe distance from it for very obvious reasons. So, if I understand that about the porcupine, why don't I practice that with the unsafe people in my life? I call them unsafe because they always manage to hurt me in some way. Whether they intend to or not, it really doesn't matter. They do, and I should practice self-protection while still extending kindness towards them. They are precious children of God as I am. However, I do not have to risk harming myself in the process. I can admire how God uses them in my life. I just need to use caution as I would with this porcupine. I never got close enough to him to get poked by the quills he had poised in my direction. Though people are very different, and I do make every effort to be friends with all, some people should not be on my hugging list. They will poke me like a porcupine and have no remorse for it.

Takeaway: Difficult people exist. It is my job in Christ to love them the best I can and know that God sees and cares about the struggle. Please God, help me to recognize the painful people early on so I can love them appropriately.

Wild Cat

Even as I please all men in all things, not seeking mine own profit, but the profit of many, that they may be saved. (I Corinthians 10:33)

My husband and I have taken several people into our home over the years. We loved each of them like family. I wish I could say it's all turned out for the best. But sadly, it's also brought many hurtful memories. I was reflecting today on one of our kiddos and I asked God, why? The kiddo we invested the most into treats us as if we were the enemy. I don't understand.

God reminded me of an adventure I had recently. I had four feral kittens that were found in my barn. I treated them all carefully and lovingly. I gave them the best care I could. I fed them and even trapped one in order to administer first aid when it had injured itself. All the while, they hissed and scratched me day after day. After some time, one of the kittens allowed me to touch her without biting and scratching at me. She began to be curious about this weird person who would sit on the barn floor tossing food and wiggling strings and feathers. Then one day it happened! I got to hold her and snuggle her! Awwww! Eventually, two more of the kittens allowed me to touch them as well. Weeks passed. But that fourth one never gave in a bit. She still scratched and bit me with fierce fury every time I attempted to love her. Why? God says to me, picture Christ. He loved and reached out to everyone. Yet some still refused and even hated him and everything that he did. All we can do is reach out and love others. We have to let them either receive us or reject us, even though it may cause wounds that hurt deeply. In the end, we really don't know how our love and outreach has affected them. We should just do our best and trust God with the outcome. PS: That wild cat never left. She had more kittens in our barn. They all love me even though their momma stays at bay.

Takeaway: You never fail when you love someone, even if they don't love you back. I pray we never fear being hurt so much that we neglect loving people.

Reflection Day

P lease take a few minutes to reflect on ways that God has revealed to you how he would like you to love other people. Maybe ways that he has burdened your heart for someone you know. This is your day to reflect, so feel free to use this page to journal whatever God has placed on your heart.

The Lord's Day

Lord, please be with us as we go to church this morning. Teach us how to love others as you do. Please show us how to look beyond the struggle and see them as you do, if even for just a moment. Everyone is precious to you. Please help us to protect our own hearts while extending love and kindness to those who may never receive us well. Please help us stop trying to hug the porcupines in our lives, but still admire the beauty and wonder they bring to life.

Week 3

Dealing with Struggles

Tumbleweeds

That we henceforth be no more children, tossed to and fro, and carried about with every wind of doctrine, by the sleight of men, and cunning craftiness, whereby they lie in wait to deceive; (Ephesians 4:14)

Tumbleweeds roll all around here. Sometimes, they will completely cover an area and make it look like a sea of dry bushes. If you have never experienced them, they are basically a weed that resembles a bush. They are prickly to the touch. They range in size from about eighteen inches to over four feet across. Unlike wood, they are lightweight and very brittle. That is how they are so easily broken free from their stem and rolled along in the wind. As they roll along, they pick up items and debris. They will most often roll along until they are trapped by something like a fence or large bush. Usually, you can just drive right over them because they will just shatter into millions of pieces. However, if there is a sea of them, you might avoid the temptation to do so. I have a love for smashing them to smithereens. One day, I drove through a wall of tumbleweeds. They had completely covered the roadway for about twenty yards! Whoo hoo! Well, there was a barbed wire fence hidden in that sea of tumbleweeds. Now I was the proud owner of four flat tires. Oops. Do you realize that some people are like these crazy weeds? They just drift through life without a plan or a care until they get caught up in something they cannot get free from. The more they fight, the more stuck they are. Think about it. We pick up habits and ideas from every source of input we allow into our lives. Then we carry them with us and struggle to change back to the way we know is right. It is extremely important that we guard ourselves from bad input. You cannot unsee things. And those images will stay with you as you go through life. God has a plan and a purpose for all of us, and it isn't to just float through each day by the seat of our pants. Stick to the plan even on tough days, and you won't get stuck with nowhere to go.

Takeaway: I should be careful not to be carried away in the whirlwind of this world. It could cause me to develop bad habits and get trapped in sin.

Recycle That Trash

A *nd we know that all things work together for good to them that love God, to them who are the called according to his purpose. (Romans 8:28)*

I cry uncontrollably at the stupidest things. Sometimes I rage. I think that nobody cares about me. That I haven't got a friend in the world. That I am all alone, unwanted, and unlovable. Am I crazy? No, I have PTSD. I've never fought in a war, but I have suffered unthinkable traumas that my subconscious brain will never forget. This means I'm broken. My life actually fell to pieces, and I was so shattered, I didn't think I would live through it. But over the years, as the pieces are being put back together, I find there are still areas that are tender and fragile. They need to be handled a little more carefully. The psychological world calls these triggers. You must put a safety on the trigger if you don't want it to be pulled. But in life, that's much easier said than done. It could be a smell, a touch, a sound, a phrase spoken, an event, a face in the crowd, or even a song on the radio that awakens the suppressed memory. The truth is that the trigger is a hidden enemy that you don't know is there until it's too late. Once triggered, I'm immediately sent back to the midst of a memory as if it was happening right now. You may try to talk to me, but I'm not reasonable at that moment. There's no fight or flight for me. It's only fight! Fight! FIGHT! I've got to survive this! I am not going to be broken again! So how do you help me? Be patient with me.

Understand I'm not really attacking you. I will come back to reality. I love you. I wouldn't hurt you. I just need to calm down and realize where I really am. God has taught me so much about myself over the years, and my triggers are much better protected.

Counseling is a strange concept. Going to talk to someone who doesn't do much except listen. But in those moments, where you can remember in a safe atmosphere, with someone who will guide you, is helpful. God can use those moments to help rewrite the memory. Give you ways to see your escape. Show you where he and his angels were during the trauma. Yes, he was there. He didn't approve, but he had a higher purpose. He brought me through so I can help others who suffer. He has allowed me to love and strengthen so many. I don't know what you may have faced in your past or even currently are facing, but understand that those events will never be good. That's not what this verse in Romans is saying. It's who we become as a result of trusting God in the midst of the trauma, that becomes good. I love you.

Takeaway: Bad things happen, horrible unspeakable things at times, but if you trust God, he will help you grow into a beautiful individual that can use the bad to make good. He will help you recycle that trash.

Gossip Goo

*B*ut the tongue can no man tame; it is an unruly evil, full of deadly poison. (James 3:8)

I had a conversation with a teenager about gossip the other day. I have played video games with my grandchildren often. In fact, I really look forward to game time with them. So, in correlation to the age of the person I was trying to console, I thought of this enemy in Super Mario games. The piranha plant. This scary, wicked plant is always trying to bite you or steal your hat. In *Super Mario Odessey*, your hat is your identity as well as your weapon, your companion, and your guide. Well, the piranha plant purposely tries to hurt you. Some are more dangerous ones that spew purple goo that injures you and slows you down so you cannot easily escape. These plants are usually in groups, so you face three, four, or even more at the same time. You must clear the goo from your path as well as shake it off yourself, while at the same time, fighting the piranha plant that is attacking you. It's no easy feat! Well, falling victim to gossip is very similar. It usually has just a bit of truth to it so others will join in and help the gossip to spread. So, one rumor can spread to several different groups of people in your church, your family, your job, and even the community! It can hurt so deeply that it slows you down into a slump of depression. Or if you are a fighter like me, you might rise in a fit of self-defense and start spewing hurtful words back at the ones hurting you. It also steals or damages your testimony in some way. If not in the gossip itself, possibly in the way you respond to it. It seems to come from everywhere at the same time too! All I can say as a Christian is if you find yourself in such a situation, remember that your identity is in Christ. Like Mario's trusty hat, Christ will clear the gossip goo and knock your enemy silly so you can safely go about your way. It may take some time. You may suffer damage. But if you trust His word and follow His way, you will find victory.

Takeaway: Don't let gossip steal your joy. Allow God to handle it. He is far more capable and cares about your happiness.

Put a Lid on That Trash

Casting all your care upon him; for he careth for you. (I Peter 5:7)

When I carry my garbage to the curb, I leave it there. The garbage man comes and takes it away. I've been doing that for years now. Not once have I ever thought that I should go ask the garbage man how my trash handled the ride to the dump. Nor have I ever thought to go visit it. Nope, once it's out, I never really think of it again. That is, unless for some reason, it doesn't get hauled off like I planned. Then I'm on the phone trying to get an explanation for why it's still there and when they will come get it. Well, God understands that we have days where life hits us hard. Some things are just too big to handle alone. He tells us to seek wise counsel. He also suggests that we talk with friends. We are designed to live in a community with one another. We draw strength and encouragement from each other. Like Aaron and Hur holding the arms of Moses during the battle against Amalek. He needed their strength and support. There was no way he could do it on his own strength. We, too, need friends and counselors to help us bear the burdens we carry at times. I have a dear friend that I can go to with my heartaches and woes. She will listen and love me without judging me. She cries with me, prays with me, and holds me when I need it. However, if I come back over and over with the same complaints, she will tell me that her ears are not garbage pails. Truthfully, this offended me the first time she said that. But she is right! I need to stop visiting my garbage. It stinks! God says to cast all our cares upon him. I don't believe he wants us to keep coming back to him over and over, asking how it's going with that burden I dumped on him yesterday. I need to treat it like that garbage can at the curb. Let it go away and never think of it again. Stop visiting the garbage!

Takeaway: I need to trust God to care about me enough to get rid of the burdens I cast upon him. I need to put a lid on the past.

Dancing in the Rain

*F*or our light affliction, which is but for a moment, worketh for us a far more exceeding and eternal weight of glory; (II Corinthians 4:17)

We've raised all kinds of animals on our farm. I loved the pigs. Yes, they were dirty and lacking in social grace. I can see why God refers to them as unclean beasts. But I loved them. They would squeal with excitement every time I came out. There was never a question as to what mood they were in. Without words, they could clearly communicate what was on their minds. Feeding time was always a frenzy. Do not get between a pig and his food! But watering time was my favorite. There was a water fountain for them to freely drink from and a small children's pool for them to wade in. I would wash out the pool every afternoon and refill it. Pigs love water! That's truly an understatement. They love it as much as food. They stayed clear of me as I cleaned the pool, but as soon as I set it down to fill it back up, they started dancing. Yes, dancing! They started by twirling in individual circles like dogs chasing their tails. Then a bit of do-si-do, two-by-two twirls, square dance style. When I got out of the pen and had the hose making water rainbows, they would dance in the rain it created while doing cannonballs into the pool. So much excitement and so much energy! When they tuckered themselves out, they would walk over to me at the fence and let me scrub the remaining dirt off them with the brush and then go to the hut to nap.

God wants us to dance in the rain too. Just like my pigs. They knew it was bath time, but the filth of life had them so weighed down that they rejoiced with dancing when the rain started. We, too, need the rejuvenation that a little down time can bring at times. You can only see rainbows on the other side of the rain. So, dance in the rain, knowing it will pass and the refreshment of the storm's passing will bring joy, sunshine, and rainbows.

Takeaway: The not so good days in life help us to appreciate the good days even more. We need them whether we realize it or not. So, we should try to make the most of them and dance while it rains.

Reflection Day

This week was about the fact that our lives are full of pain and struggles. Can you spend a few minutes reflecting on how God has helped you to find joy, peace, or added strength in the struggles you have?

The Lord's Day

Our Heavenly Father, thank you so much for never leaving us alone in the hardships this life brings upon us. Even though we may not recognize your presence in our trials, we know you are there because you promised you would be. I pray we continue to learn to draw from your strength so that we don't linger in pain and heartache. Help us find joy.

Week 4

Reaching Others

What Are You Doing?

L *et your light so shine before men, that they may see your good works,* *and glorify your Father which is in heaven. (Matthew 5:16)*

Today was a day of reflection for me. And as I sat here, I thought of all the children God has blessed me with. My biological ones, my adopted ones, my Sunday school kids, camp kids, neighbor kids, all of them. There must be thousands of them! One very special memory came back to me today from when we lived in Gig Harbor. We lived in a trailer court full of children. I took all of them to church and AWANAS and hiking or wherever I went. I even took them grocery shopping with me. My regular cashier truly thought that I had ten children. I loved them, and they knew it. They were constantly bringing me gifts and helping me with whatever I needed to do. Not easy tasks either. They would spend all day cleaning my gutters, weeding my garden, mopping my floors, whatever I needed.

One day, one of the kids' moms came to visit me and asked me why she must bake cookies for me. I was puzzled of course, so she explained that her daughter insisted that she had to bake cookies for me so she could mop my floor. I had said that's what I was going to do that day. She further explained that she could hardly get her to pick up a broom without a fight, but she insists on helping me! "What are you doing?" She asked. That's a great question! Serving God isn't glamorous. Yet if we do it right, others are drawn into joining us.

I think I've grown tired over the years. I'm slacking on showing how happy I really am to have a Lord that loves me so much. What am I doing?!?!? Let's all get back to that place where others are excited to be with us. Where they will join in to do whatever menial tasks we are doing, just so they can experience that love and acceptance only God can give.

Takeaway: If you let God's love shine through you, others will be drawn to Him. Let your light shine!

Friendly Banter

*B*e kindly affectioned one to another with brotherly love; in honour
preferring one another; (Romans 12:10)

I had a little friendly fight with my son this morning. He's retired from
the military, and he's going through quite a bit with his PTSD and trying
to learn how to live in society again. He's been downhearted for a few days
now, and I've been praying for him.

This morning, I felt like picking a fight with him. His bedroom door was
open, and he was sitting in his chair, reading. I walked right up to him and
pointed my finger at him and aggressively said, "I just want you to know,
that I love you!" He looked at me, confused.

So, I said even more aggressively, "And there's nothing you can do about
it, see?!? You're just going to have to accept that fact and live with it!"

To which he responded with great energy, while jumping to his feet and
towering over me, "Oh yeah? Why?"

I said, "Because that's the way it is! Got it?"

This banter went on for several moments, getting louder, and louder. It
got loud enough to concern my husband who was sleeping at the other end
of the house. It was 6:00 in the morning.

My son needed to release some of the pent-up frustration he was feeling. Friendly banter doesn't hurt anybody, and it can be quite fun. And in this moment, it was what he needed. It ended up with him telling me, "Well, let me just say this, I love you too! So take that!" We hugged and laughed. My son has been singing for the last half hour. Oh, how that warms my heart.

Paul says in *1 Corinthians 9:22*, *"I am made all things to all men, that I might by all means save some".* That includes our own households, ladies. Figure out what your kids and your husband need from you, then reach out to them in their love language. Those few moments that I spent fake fighting with my son told him that I really see him. It told him that I get what he's going through. It also told him that I truly love him. So reach out to your family and friends. Even if it's just friendly banter.

Takeaway: Sometimes we need to adjust the manner in which we communicate love to our friends and family. Just saying the words isn't enough at times. Put your love into action.

Falling Rocks

Let the word of Christ dwell in you richly in all wisdom; teaching and admonishing one another in psalms and hymns and spiritual songs, singing with grace in your hearts to the Lord. (Colossians 3:16)

Such a beautiful day, such a beautiful time we had with our friends. And then it happened! We were driving home and were crossing a beautiful mountain pass when we were faced with a rockslide. Our friends were following behind us in their little VW Rabbit. There wasn't any time to avoid the collision. We struck a rock that made a horrible sound as it went under our Buick. The car bounced left and right and up and down. It had our attention! All we knew was that it hit hard, and we were afraid to stop until we could actually get off the road. There was nowhere to stop on the mountain pass as there's only two narrow lanes and a big cliff. As the car started to make noise, we turned it off and just coasted down the mountainside until we approached a restaurant where we could pull over.

My husband threw a black T-shirt over his white dress shirt and laid down to assess the situation. It wasn't good. The rock had torn the bottom of our radiator, ripped across the oil pan, and our transfer case was leaking. In other words, there wasn't a drop of fluid left in our engine, and we were going nowhere. Well, the men thought maybe they would rush back to the house. It was only an hour and a half away. They could come right back and get me, my friend, and our five children. That meant a minimum of three and a half to four hours that we would be standing outside because the restaurant was closing. Yes, it was that time of day and in the mountains at night it gets rather chilly and there are wild animals. We decided that probably wasn't the best course of action. Instead, in our great wisdom, we decided to pile all nine of us into that little VW Rabbit. That made for another great adventure of the day.

We were singing and telling stories when a police officer pulled us over. He looked in the car and saw my husband in his black T-shirt and white dress shirt combination. He must have thought he was a Catholic priest. He looked at all of us. He looked at my husband. He shook his head and said while chuckling, "Drive carefully". He saw a super saint driving all of us home in his tiny little car! We had so much fun at the fellowship meeting and even though this horrible thing happened to our car, what a wonderful memory it was. Our friends and our children will never forget how we handled that adversity. You know, bad things happen to everybody and how we handle it is so important. Other people are watching, and they are experiencing our attitude in times of trouble. What are you teaching people as you face the trials of life? Do they see Jesus even when times are hard for you?

Takeaway: Bad things happen to good people and good people just keep going.

I Can Be Useful

Withal praying also for us, that God would open unto us a door of utterance, to speak the mystery of Christ, for which I am also in bonds: (Colossians 4:3)

I don't have a lot of confidence. I freak out when I have to talk in front of people. I admire people that can stand up at the pulpit and speak as if they are in their living room with family. How do they do this? Are they the only ones God can use? How could he use a weakling like me? I have committed to do what God asks me to do. I have been asked a few times to speak at ladies' conferences. I know my lessons would've been so much better if I wasn't so terrified. However, don't discount how God uses me to reach others. The fact that I stood there in total fear and trusting God to see me through encouraged others that they, too, could be used to reach out beyond their own comfort zone. No, I don't believe I will ever be a great speaker. But I will not tell God, no. I will do what he asks me to do. I must trust that he knows what is best for me and for those he has brought to me. It is amazing to hear testimony of how the little things we do affect others.

I was honored to speak at a Mother's Day banquet a few years ago in a town several hours away. When my hubby and I were out on a weekend away, we stopped in that church I spoke at to worship on Sunday. I had forgotten my lesson and even being there for that banquet. A sweet lady came up to me and proceeded to tell me how much that message touched her life. She has treasured the thoughts and encouragement for years. She further stated that she teaches her children these nuggets of truth as well. I was shocked to say the least. I really felt inadequate and like I had let God down with my inability. But he was able to take my weakness and use it to build strength in this dear lady. So, never think too lowly of yourself. God can and will use whatever ability you have to encourage and reach others for his glory.

Takeaway: What a joy it is to look back and see that even a timid, unskilled, wallflower like me can have an impact in this world. Let God use you too.

I'm Honored

And the publican, standing afar off, would not lift up so much as his eyes unto heaven, but smote upon his breast, saying, God be merciful to me a sinner. I tell you, this man went down to his house justified rather than the other: for every one that exalteth himself shall be abased;and he that humbleth himself shall be exalted. (Luke 18:13-14)

I have several adopted children. One, I have a signed adoption certificate for. It's not legal, but that's a story for another day. His mother was involved in a terrible car accident, and her healing process was quite intense. During those dark days, her son came to stay with us quite often. He was one of our children's best friends, so it was just natural for him to be with us. As the years passed by, he grew to be like a brother to all the others and a son to me. Well, the day came when he found the lady he wanted to marry. Of course, I was going to the wedding. So, when I arrived, I wondered where I would be sitting. I noticed all the seats up front and thought, well I am his adopted mother, am I supposed to sit up there with the family? Everybody was so busy preparing for the wedding that I didn't want to disturb anybody by asking such a petty question. So, I decided I would sit in the back on the groom's side with the other guests and friends.

He arrived and walked his mother down to the honored seat up front, then he turned and began scanning the crowd, looking for somebody. I didn't know who until he walked up to me and said, "There you are."

Then he took me by the hand and said, "You should be sitting up here since you're my mother."

I said, "But your real mother is there, that's her seat."

He said, "You're my real mother too." How honored I was that he loved me as much as I loved him. But can you imagine if I had sat there just assuming that was my right and the opposite had been true? What if he had seen me sitting there and said, "I'm sorry, but that seat was reserved for my aunt, could you please move to the back?" I would have been humiliated and heartbroken.

The Bible is true in every way. God tells us in these verses that it is better to behave with humility. That way we will be honored at times like this. Yes, I was ugly crying before the wedding even began because of how he honored me. I hope he has a special memory of that moment too.

Takeaway: In choosing to humble myself, I allowed my son the blessing of honoring me. It was a win-win for both of us. Choose humility.

Reflection Day

Write some ways in which you allowed God to use you to reach others this week. How were you able to use your everyday activities to invite others to feel loved and invited?

The Lord's Day

Lord, we are so small and insignificant. Yet, we know you have a purpose for each of us. Please help us to be willing to step beyond our comfort to be a blessing and encouragement to those you bring into our lives. Each and every soul is so precious to you and needs to be treated as such. Please help us to honor you in all we say and do.

Week 5

God Completes Me

Déjà vu

*T*he secret things belong unto the LORD our God: but those things which are revealed belong unto us and to our children for ever, that we may do all the words of this law (Deuteronomy 29:29)

Have you ever experienced déjà vu? That time when you just know that you've already lived this day or this moment. The memory is so real, and it feels so surreal to be living a memory. In encouraging others let's not forget how God encourages us. One particular way that sticks out in my mind today is this déjà vu. I've experienced it many times, especially during my depression. I've come to believe that these are moments when God wants me to remember that he already knew my future. While living in this memory right now, he's reminding me that he saw this day coming and he prepared me for it. He's been with me every step of the way just like he promised.

I had one of these moments just the other day. I have worked at the post office for twenty-five years now. I had been on my favorite route for over ten years when I had a dream that I would be on the route I am currently on. I have never wanted this route. But I remember vividly that I dreamed I was assigned this route and that a certain address that was not on it at the time of the dream was now a part of this route too. I told one of my coworkers my dream, and he laughed at me. There was no way that address would be on his route. That was as funny as thinking that I would have his route for myself. Well, here I am fifteen years later, and I not only have his route, but that address is also on the route. I stood there the other day holding a piece of mail for that address and the déjà vu began. I remembered that letter! I remembered the next several moments that occurred after that too! I remembered the conversation taking place on the workroom floor. The clothes I was wearing. EVERYTHING! God knew this day was coming. It is comforting to know that no matter what's going on, God already knew, and he loves me enough to stay here with me and see me through.

Takeaway: God knows my yesterdays, my todays, and all my tomorrows. He is with me every step of the way and gives me gentle reminders to keep me focused. He wants me to know that he is here.

The Missing Piece

*E*ven every one that is called by my name: for I have created him for my glory, I have formed him; yea, I have made him. (Isaiah 43:7)

I love puzzles! My favorite one is a 1500-piece mosaic of Mickey Mouse. The creator of this puzzle put together a picture of Mickey Mouse from photos of scenes from the classic Disney movies. This puzzle is so very intricate that it comes with a poster of the completed mosaic so you can look closely at which scenes form the picture. My daughter and I toiled over it for several days and FINALLY it was finished! However, there was a piece missing!!! Nothing worse than that. I couldn't frame it with a piece missing. Oh, I showed it off for a while on our table. But everyone noticed the missing piece. It was right in the center of Mickey's eye. How could you miss it? This is a one-of-a-kind puzzle too. It's not replaceable. Bummer of bummers.

Well, we are all one-of-a-kind creations. God created us as unique individuals. Most don't have trouble acknowledging that. He created us for a purpose. That purpose brings glory to Him. However, if we don't accept Christ as our Savior, we have a piece missing. It's like there's a hole (or void if you prefer) in our heart, but we really don't understand what it is. So, we search for it in all the wrong places. Many become promiscuous. Others drink or do drugs. There are so many ways we try to fill the void in our hearts. But until we ask Christ to come into our heart and save us from our sins, our search is in vain. When we allow Christ to come into our life, He fills the emptiness. The missing pieces of our life are found and start to fall into place.

Takeaway: We are created by Jesus for Jesus and until we accept Jesus, we will be incomplete.

Pruning

Every branch in me that beareth not fruit he taketh away: and every branch that beareth fruit, he purgeth it, that it may bring forth more fruit. (John 15:2)

Living in this valley has taught me a lot about orchard work. I watch as the trees begin to bud in the spring; their branches shooting forth and the leaves coming out. They're growing so fast! Then the workers come in and prune everything back. Well, that doesn't stop these little trees. They begin to bloom. The flowers are everywhere, and they're just beautiful with color. Again, they're reaching forth branches and filling up with leaves and looking so full and growing so fast! Then the workers come and prune them again. They still don't stop. The trees start to put forth their fruit. They've got so many apples, peaches, or cherries all over their branches. Their fruit is overloading them! They're the most fruitful trees I have ever seen. Then the workers come and pick off half the fruit. Maybe even more than half!

You know, this is how I feel in my Christian Walk sometimes. I'm gung-ho and go forward all the way. Working working working. Trying to win souls. Trying to get people to church. Teaching my lessons. Doing everything I can for God. Yet somebody keeps cutting me down or something's stopping my work, or something happens to where it just feels like I'm getting nowhere though I'm trying so hard. Why? Well, I have learned that the workers prune the trees and keep their branches thinner so that the sunlight can get to the fruit. This helps the fruit to have a more even color making it prettier. By pulling off half the fruit or even more, you get larger fruit. This also allows for more nutrients in the fruit. So, all this pruning that the trees go through is to improve the quality of the fruit they produce. It's the same with my Christian Walk. The struggles and trials and the difficulties that I face just help me do a better job. They help me struggle to find a better way. And let's remember that others are watching and may benefit from my growth. My fruit is improving whether I notice it or not, and I am grateful to the Lord.

Takeaway: The struggles I face in my spiritual growth are building character in me that will allow me to be a more productive Christian.

The Ruts of Life

*A*s far as the east is from the west, so far hath he removed our transgressions from us. (Psalm 103:12)

Life is full of choices and those choices direct the path of our life. I remember my dad having a heart-to-heart with me as I was becoming an adult. He pulled out a photo his dad had given him at the same point in his life. The photo was of a sign on the Oregon trail. It was a tin photo that dated way back to the days of the wagon train. The sign stood in the middle of a fork in the trail and read: Choose your rut wisely. You will be in it for about forty miles. Today, it doesn't take long to travel forty miles. But back then, it could have taken several days to travel that far. My husband watches a lot of western documentaries, and I've seen horror stories of how these ruts tore apart wagons and caused pain and suffering to the people inside the wagons. What my father wanted me to understand is that each choice I make in my life will take me down a path of consequence. Some consequences can last a long time, maybe even my whole life. Other consequences may not have much impact on me at all but may affect the ones I love. Choices need to be made with prayer and thoughtfulness.

The other thought he imparted to me was that only the people who were hauling stuff they couldn't part with had to deal with these ruts. They had baggage from their past that they wouldn't leave behind to start this new life.

That's why they needed a wagon to carry it all in. He wanted me to understand that if I really want to move ahead in life; I need to let the past stay in the past. Stop trying to haul it with me everywhere I go. Unforgiveness can cause a burden so heavy that it will bog me down into a rut I may never get freed from. Christ gave me a new start when he saved me from my sins. He has forgiven me for all my past sins. So, doesn't it make sense that I should forgive myself too? Stop carrying the shame and guilt of a past I've been forgiven of and move forward into the new life I have been offered? Furthermore, I should also extend that same forgiving grace to those who have wronged me.

Takeaway: God doesn't want us to live in the past. He has forgotten it and put it as far as the east is from the west. We should learn to let it go and live uninhibited by the baggage of our past.

Peculiar?

*B*ut ye are a chosen generation, a royal priesthood, an holy nation, a peculiar people; that ye should shew forth the praises of him who hath called you out of darkness into his marvellous light: (1 Peter 2:9)

I have a pair of sewing scissors that my hubby gave me for my birthday a very long time ago. I used to sew to bring in extra money for groceries or trips to see our parents. He would watch me struggle with cheap pairs and see how much they hurt my hands to use. So, he bought me a very expensive pair of sewing shears. Well, these shears are off-limits to anyone except me. I keep them in the sheath and safe and only use them on fabric or thread. Any time I need them, I know exactly where to find them, and they are always sharp and up to the task even after more than thirty years and never having been sharpened. There have been times when I would catch someone pulling them out to use, and I would quickly put a stop to that notion! These are mine. They are special. They are for fabric only; no paper or anything else is to ever touch their blades. Don't get me wrong, I do share them when someone is sewing with me, but I hope you get the point.

Well, God calls us a peculiar people. According to today's definition, that means we are weird or different. But back in ancient days, it meant, purchased for a special use. So, if we look at that phrase again in this context; we were purchased by God, with the blood of Christ, for a special use. We have a purpose and a unique place in His plan. And, just like my sewing shears, God wants us to be ready and up for the task when He calls on us. We are given guidelines in his word to show us how to protect ourselves from the temptation of sin. In this way, we stay sharp. If we allow ourselves to be drawn away into the world, we become dull to any spiritual use. So, stay in the protective sheath of God's love and his word. Don't allow yourself to be used for any other purpose than what He has purchased you for. You are precious to him.

Takeaway: We are so precious to God that he purchased us at a very high price. We should do the best we possibly can to keep ourselves solely for His use.

Reflection Day

Today, as you reflect on how God treasures you, can you write a few ways that he has revealed to you how much he loves you? Maybe write some ways that he has reminded you of his presence in your life.

The Lord's Day

Precious Lord, thank you so much for being there for us. It is so comforting to know that you already know what is coming in our tomorrows. Help us to trust you and lean on you as we go through this life. If you see fit, Lord, please help us to reach out and encourage someone today.

Week 6

Let Us Pray

My Prayer Acronym

A nd it came to pass, that, as he was praying in a certain place, when he ceased, one of his disciples said unto him, Lord, teach us to pray, as John also taught his disciples. (Luke 11:1)

The disciples asked Jesus to teach them to pray. Prayer is such an important act of faith. We pray because we believe that he's listening to us, or at the very least, we hope he is. Either way, we believe he's there. Because it's one of the first acts in our faith, I thought the acronym of acts is appropriate for learning to pray.

Pray in   A   Adoration of who God is.

Pray in   C   Confession of who you are.

Pray in   T   Thanksgiving for all He does.

Pray in   S   Supplication for your needs.

God is holy, righteous, all-powerful, all-knowing, loving, and so much more! He is worthy of all the praise we can give him. It's only fitting that we start our prayers acknowledging who he is. We owe him our respect. Furthermore, we should remember who we are. We are his creation. We should always be humble to the fact of our own sin nature and failings too. We are instructed to confess our faults, to seek forgiveness daily. When we put ourselves into a humble state, we are more likely to be grateful for the mercy and grace that he extends to us each and every moment of our lives. We will have a thankful heart. He supplies our every need even before we ask him. He loves to hear us talk to Him. Finally, ask him for whatsoever thing you need or desire. Take note of his answers. Even if his answer is no, it is what is best so be thankful.

Takeaway: We should pray in a way that honors God and expresses how grateful we are that he listens and answers our humble prayers. Prayer is our direct line to the heart of God.

Learning to Pray

I love the LORD, because he hath heard my voice and my supplications. (Psalm 116:1)

I remember as a child; I would go to my daddy and tell him I needed his help with a problem. He would sit down and ask me to tell him all about it. He would ask me what I've already tried to do to solve this problem on my own. He would hardly say a word as I would cry and tell him all my heart. Finally, he would throw me some helpful ideas, or some tidbits of wisdom, and I would receive it all gladly. My daddy was helping me, and I knew my problem would be solved! God is our Heavenly Father. Unfortunately, most of us approach him in our prayers as if we are giving him a shopping list. Lord, help me with this, or Lord, I need that. Even when we include others in our prayer list, it is still in the same manner. Do we forget that he is our Heavenly Father? Do we forget that he is always there, listening to our cries? Do we forget that he knows infinitely more than we can even imagine? How frustrated would we be if our children treated us in such a manner as that? God wants us to talk to him as we would our biological father. He loves us and wants to commune with us. So instead of offering up a list, maybe we could talk to him. "Lord, I'm struggling with a problem right now. I really need your insight on how to handle it." Tell him all your thoughts, dreams, fears. Then stop. Listen to the soft whisper he implants in your heart. Receive his wisdom. Most importantly, respond in action like you would if your daddy gave you the ideas.

Takeaway: The Lord loves us and hears our prayers. He wants to help us with our problems as well as share in our joys. We should talk to Him, not just throw him our wish lists.

Little Prayers

Train up a child in the way he should go: and when he is old, he will not depart from it. (Proverbs 22:6)

Every night before bed, I would talk with my children. It was part of our winding down process. We would sit and enjoy a cup of hot chocolate, or a bowl of popcorn or such, and they would tell me all about how their day went. I would hear tattling, complaints, or many times, I would hear them regale the great and exciting things that happened that day. Then we would head off to brush our teeth and settle into bed where I would tuck them in, then talking with them and praying with them individually. I miss that now that they are grown. I wish I knew back then just how important this ritual was to all of us.

Our children need to learn how to pray. They need to learn to recognize answered prayer. They need to see and recognize God working in their lives. It is so very important that they learn to trust and turn to God for themselves. Not just because Mommy and Daddy turn to prayer for them. So many times, we pray for our children. This isn't wrong. But they also need to learn to lift up their own voices to God. To say their own little prayers. They need to learn that they can turn to him when they are scared or hurting. They need to learn to praise Him and be thankful for his protection and provision in their lives. And most important of all, they need to call on him to save them from their sins. As much as we love our children, they must call on God themselves. We cannot do it for them. Please, lead and guide your children in prayer. Teach them this freedom they have. They need to know that they can approach the King of Kings and Lord of Lords with their hearts. In time, they will teach your grandchildren to do so as well.

Takeaway: The little prayers of our children are so very important and so very precious to God. We need to be diligent in teaching our children how to talk to God.

Pray for Others

Bear ye one another's burdens, and so fulfil the law of Christ. (Galatians 6:2)
I have a dear friend who is now home with the Lord. But I have a very special memory of a time we shared. Our ladies' group always puts together a Christmas box for someone that God placed in our hearts. We would pray over her and prepare for her most of the year. Sometime in February or early March, I was burdened for my friend and shared my heart with the ladies' group. Her husband was the Pastor of a church in a town about two hours away. My husband invited them to come and minister to our people so they could get to know her for themselves as well. I began to crochet a blanket for her. It was a difficult pattern and had many different colors. It took me the better part of the next nine months to finish it. I wasn't sure I would get it done in time but God blessed my work and it was beautiful. The day came when my husband and I went to visit my friend and her husband at their home to give her the box the ladies and I had put together for her. She was reluctant to accept our visit. Turns out that her mother had passed away two weeks before, and she wasn't in a good place emotionally. But being the gracious lady she was, she put on her best face and came out to greet us. I presented her with our heartfelt gift. As she sat there opening it and removing each piece individually, she got to the blanket at the bottom of the box and exclaimed, "Did you make this for me?" I assured her

I had. That it was a true labor of love since it was much more difficult than I anticipated. She sat there in tears and hugging it closely to her heart. Then she shared with us how her mother had passed and how her heart was so depressed over the loss. Seeing the work it took to make this blanket told her that God knew she was going to struggle through this holiday. That he loved her so much that he had a group of ladies toiling in prayer over her for months to help her through. How that blessed my heart! All I knew until that moment was that I thought of her a lot and knew she needed prayer. I don't know how often, but I know I prayed and prayed that God would bless her and hold her and remind her that she is loved. My dear friend, pray for people when God brings them to your mind. You never know just how much they may be needing you, even from afar.

Takeaway: God lays people on our hearts. We may see their face in a crowd or just have their name on our mind. In whatever manner he does it, pray for them. You never know how much they may need it at that moment.

Give Thanks

Giving thanks always for all things unto God and the Father in the name of our Lord Jesus Christ; (Ephesians 5:20)

In all things, give thanks, but it's not easy. We used to live in Wichita. The weather there was so unpredictable. I remember I had gone to the store for some groceries one day and the wind started to pick up and it was starting to rain. It rained hard! I didn't have a car. I was given permission to use a shopping cart as long as I promised to keep it in a safe place and bring it back. The manager was so good to me. I would go in the store often and volunteer to do mystery shopping for him so he could deliver groceries to the elderly who were unable to drive themselves any longer. On this particular day, I felt the need to turn down a road I never usually travelled. It was a longer route, but I felt very strongly that I should. A quiet voice in my head kept urging that I needed to go the extra half mile out of my way. I obeyed. My young son didn't mind. He liked seeing new things. But it was windy, and I was being pelted by the rain, so I jogged the best I could while pushing the shopping cart. My son was squealing all the way. He thought this was a fun game! A couple hours later, my neighbor came over to visit and asked if I had heard about what happened on that street I was told to avoid by the voice in my head. I hadn't. We didn't have a tv either. Turns out, that sudden turn in the weather was a small tornado! It ripped down that street and tore it up! I hadn't noticed since I had my face down to try to avoid the pain of running in driving rain. Praise the Lord! He guided and protected me and my son. He kept us from possibly being killed by the flying debris this small tornado created. Oh, I wasn't too thankful for his urging me to go the long way when the weather was so bad, but I was singing his praises when I learned how he delivered me from the danger I had put myself in. Yes, in all things give thanks. Even if you are running in the middle of a tornado.

Takeaway: It may not seem right to be thankful for trials and extra burdens. But God knows what he is doing. Follow his lead and be thankful that he is there all the way.

Reflection Day

1. In the past week, have you noticed any changes in the way you pray?

2. Do you feel more comfortable approaching God in prayer?

3. In what ways have you seen answers to your prayers?

4. Can you think of a way to thank God for a struggle this week?

5. Have you been burdened to pray for anyone else this week?

The Lord's Day

Lord, as we go to worship you today, please open our hearts to receive what you have to say to us. Please help us to be in an attitude of prayer at all times, so we can hear you when you speak to us in that "still small voice". Lord, help us be receptive of your instruction and guidance, even if it is inconvenient. And Lord, help us remember to lift others up before you sincerely in our prayers. AMEN

Week 7

Stepping in the Light

The Back Side of Rainbows

Whereby are given unto us exceeding great and precious promises: that by these ye might be partakers of the divine nature, having escaped the corruption that is in the world through lust. (II Peter 1:4)

Have you ever been so close to a rainbow that you felt you could touch it? There was an extremely gloomy week last spring where it rained and rained. The clouds were so thick, it actually made the days and nights blur together. Well, a huge fire broke out on the ridge in town and my hubby and I were there to see it, so we drove by to see which direction it was spreading. Our farm is on the other side of that hillside. We also have several friends who live on both sides of this ridge. As we were driving on the road parallel to the ridge, a small rainbow formed. It seemed to be only about two miles wide at the bottom and arched right over the road we were driving on. It was the brightest rainbow I had ever seen! There were actually three of them. One on top of the other. Of course, I pulled out my camera to take pictures. The sky was bright as daylight on the side of the rainbow we were on and dark like twilight on the other side of it. This made it look even more stunning. It was still sprinkling softly while we passed under it and the rain was similar to little rainbow dew drops, like in a movie! I was so thrilled by this spectacle! I rolled my window down and hung my head out to continue taking photos. I wanted to see what the back side of a rainbow looked like. I thought it would be cool to have a picture of a rainbow with the sun in the center of it. But the rainbow was gone! I asked my hubby to circle around and pass through it again. We did, and this time I took a video of the phenomenon, but I got the same result.

Well, rainbows are a sign of a promise made by God himself. This is why they are so awe inspiring. So, it makes sense that you have to be on the right side to see it. As the sunlight was coming from behind us, we could see this dazzling display. But as we turned and faced the sun, it was invisible to us, and all that we saw was the setting sun. Well, me being me, I sat there in awe and wonder. I asked God to explain to my heart what I was witnessing. He is so good at doing that if I sit and listen. I had a sense of being held by my loving heavenly father. He showed me that he has my back. That I am his child sitting on his knee, and he is telling me that he loves me and is reminding me of his precious promises. But if I wander away, and get on the other side of his protection, those promises I hold so dear today, I may forget tomorrow. He wants me to be close to him. He wants me to trust him.

Takeaway: I should stay in close fellowship with God, my heavenly father, at all times. He has my back and never forgets his promises. If I am close, he can bring those promises to light for me to see and wonder at.

Gray Wolf

I am come a light into the world, that whosoever believeth on me should not abide in darkness. (John 12:46)

I think there's a point in every child's life where they are afraid of the dark. Well, to combat this fear, we would play a game we called Gray Wolf. We only played in the light of a full moon. There were very few rules. I explained to the children that the things in the dark are the same things in the daylight, they just look like shadows because they lack color when there's no light. But these things, like trees and carports and fences, are still solid and real and can hurt you. So, rule #1, no running. The children were to hide, and I would look for them. If they could sneak back to the porch before I found them and shined my flashlight on them, they would howl and say, Gray Wolf! Rule #2, no flashlights, except mine, of course. To be truthful, I never searched hard because rule #3 was that they had to stay within the boundaries we all agreed upon. This way, they were close by. I just wanted them to be confident that they had victory over darkness. Isn't that what Christ offers us? Victory over sin and the darkness of this world. We have to be careful as we live this life, knowing that our enemy is real. He is trying to tear us down and keep us from living victoriously. But Christ is there. His light is shining in the darkness to guide us. He promised to never leave us or forsake us. He also promised to be our light in the darkness. If we feel overwhelmed, or if we fall, we can call out and he will be there. His light will give us clear vision. We don't have to fear the darkness of this world. Satan is a defeated foe, and we have the victory in our Lord, Jesus Christ!

Takeaway: I am frightened by the horrible things I see in the world these days. But Christ has promised to be there. He will be my light in the darkness. Satan will not defeat me because I am saved.

The Glow Worm

A *nd when Aaron and all the children of Israel saw Moses, behold, the skin of his face shown; and they were afraid to come nigh him. (Exodus 34:30)*

In Exodus 34, Moses met with God on Mt Sinai. He was on the mount for forty days in communion with God as God gave him the Ten Commandments. Moses fasted the entire time he was there! He must have been so enthralled in his visit with God. Anyway, when he came down to tell the people what God had shared with him, they were afraid of him. Why? Because his face was shining! He had been so close to God that the light of God was literally shining out of him in a visible way! When I tell this story to children, I like to use a visual aid. I have a little glow worm. He is a stuffed toy that looks like a bookworm with a plastic face. When I get to the part where Moses comes to talk to the congregation, I squeeze his tummy, and his face lights up! The children usually gasp with excitement. But my little glow worm isn't frightening. He's comforting. He offers a soft glow to chase away the darkness. I can only imagine how frightening it must have been to see a real person glowing in the darkness! I imagine they paid close attention to what Moses had to share with them. The light of God shining out into their dark hearts was frightening, so Moses covered his face with a veil to dim it for their comfort. Thinking about it, angels are in the presence of God, and they glow all over! Even their clothing glows with the light of God! How precious to be in the presence of God. You know, others do notice when we are in close fellowship with our Lord. Even if our faces don't shine like a glow worm.

Takeaway: I want to be so close to God that others notice! I want to let God's radiance be seen through my life.

A Dozen Flashlights

Yea, though I walk through the valley of the shadow of death, I will fear no evil: for thou art with me; thy rod and thy staff they comfort me. Thou preparest a table before me in the presence of mine enemies: thou anointest my head with oil; my cup runneth over. Surely goodness and mercy shall follow me all the days of my life: and I will dwell in the house of the LORD for ever. (Psalm 23:4-6)

Thanksgiving is my favorite holiday. It's a day where we can get together with the ones we love and just play games, hang out, and eat until we nearly explode. One year, I had planned some games to play in the dark with all my grandchildren. They were rather young at the time. So I went and bought a dozen flashlights and plenty of batteries. Well, in the middle of the afternoon, a drunk driver came rocketing down the road and veered off, hitting our mailbox and a telephone pole that sent him airborne into the neighbor's front room! This changed all our plans for a while. The neighbor, for obvious reasons, but the rest of the neighborhood was without power since he took out the pole with the transformer box at the top of it. Dinner wasn't an issue for us since I have always cooked the turkey overnight, so my oven would be free for baking rolls and pies and whatever else. However, my plans for all those flashlights was now a topic of discussion. The time was just after noon, so we had a while before we needed to be concerned, but preparations needed to be made. It turned out to be such a fun night! We decided to just let the kids have the lights as I originally planned. They ran all over the house searching for each other in hide and seek as well as searching for items in scavenger hunts. There were beams of light everywhere in the house that night. The children were disappointed the next day when the power was restored.

Isn't it amazing how God can transform a serious inconvenience into a precious memory? Through the prayers offered in preparation for this time, He delivered us. He gave the idea of playing flashlight games weeks before. Everything we needed was already in place when the tragedy struck. Our neighbor was able to rebuild in a short time and none of them were injured since they were away visiting family.

How marvelous to look back and see how God had prepared us and protected us.

Takeaway: It's always amazing to see how God prepares us and protects us. Even more amazing how He can take what appears to be a horrible day and turn it into a day full of beautiful memories to cherish.

A Victorious Attitude

For I am not ashamed of the gospel of Christ: for it is the power of God unto salvation to every one that believeth; to the Jew first, and also to the Greek. (Romans 1:16)

Years of Little League games have left their mark on me. I have spent summer after summer in the bleachers. I noticed something though. Even though the kids were all good sports for the most part, there was a definite difference in attitude after winning a game as opposed to losing. After a loss, they would still go shake the hands of the opposing team and tell them it was a good game. Afterwards, they would come back to the dugout with a non-energetic attitude and offer encouragement to their own teammates that struggled that day. If they won the game, I'm sure you can imagine the excitement and rejoicing these little characters would display. These attitudes would carry on through the week at practices. They would either be building each other up or bragging about the great plays of the last game. I need to learn from this display.

As a born-again believer, I have victory over sin and the grave. Christ has won the battle for me. I have bragging rights, so to say. Then why do I shy away in a moment of witness? Why am I afraid of what people think of me? I am the victor because I am on team Jesus! I need to keep an attitude of humility, remembering all Christ has done for me. But I must also remember to keep my chin up in confidence. I am not defeated, nor should I behave like I am. My children would never be ashamed to claim what team they are on after a championship win. Therefore, why am I? This victory that Christ has given me is far more precious than any other championship I could imagine winning. I am not ashamed of Christ! Let's go share the gospel!

Takeaway: I should never be ashamed to tell others of the gospel of Christ that gave me the greatest of all victories.

Reflection Day

Since the darkness of sin is evident all around us, how were you able to find victory in the struggles of your world?

The Lord's Day

Lord, please help us to be bold and confident in the gospel you have given us. It truly is our prayer that our loved ones and friends get to share the joys of heaven with us, so please help us to share with them. Please help us to share with those whom you bring our way, without fear. There is nothing to be ashamed of and all judgment belongs to you alone. You are the only one we truly need to please. Thank you for everything.

Week 8

God Loves Children

The Faith of a Child

A *nd said, Verily I say unto you, Except ye be converted, and become as little children, ye shall not enter into the kingdom of heaven. (Matthew 18:3)*

There was a man who lived a house away and down the hill from us. He was an overseas airline pilot so he was hardly ever home. One day I heard my six-year-old son calling for me and as I stepped outside to see what was going on, there he was, walking up the hill, with my son by his side, and he was carrying a television. My son excitedly pointed at me and squealed, "There she is! That's my mom!"

Well, it turns out that this man's TV had broken, and he was setting it out to the curb for the garbage man to pick up when my son convinced him that his mom can fix anything. The man proceeded to tell me that I was under no obligation, but if I could fix it, he would greatly appreciate it. Let's be honest, I had never fixed a television or anything electronic in my life. I knew precious little about electronics. I hardly knew how to operate the remote control, but my young son was convinced that I could do anything. Therefore, I was at least going to try.

We set the TV on my workstation (otherwise known as the kitchen cabinet). My son ran to get my toolbox, and we set to work taking the TV apart. That was the easy part! Once we got inside of it, the children and I looked at it and were overwhelmed by the number of thing-a-ma-bobs in there. That's technical jargon for 'I didn't know what I was looking at.' I looked at my son, and the crowd of gathering children, and suggested that we pray and ask God to reveal the problem to us. Sure enough, right after we prayed, I saw it! There was a very tiny wire that was broken. Some mouse droppings were right beside the fractured wire, so I assume the little feller nibbled it. I asked my little assistant to hand me the soldering iron and wire, and we gently soldered the ends back together. After another inspection, we decided that was the only visible problem and closed the back of the television for testing. IT WORKED!!! IT REALLY WORKED! I will never forget how relieved I felt and how joyously the children all ran down the hill to retrieve my neighbor. They were shouting the news all the way! She fixed it! She fixed it! But I didn't fix it. God fixed it! Through the faith of a child, he showed me that I can believe in His abilities as much as my little boy believed in mine. To be more candid, I should believe in God's abilities far more than that. He is unlimited.

Takeaway: Yes, through prayer and the faith of a child, God used my hands to fix a TV. What else does he have planned for me if I trust him?

Tuck and Roll

*T*rain up a child in the way he should go: and when he is old, he will not depart from it. (Proverbs 22:6)

The gutters were packed with leaves, moss, and pine needles. They needed cleaning desperately, but I am terrified of heights. How was I going to accomplish this? Well, I pulled out the ladder and leaned it against the carport and did a most pathetic stretch and throw tactic. It only took a few minutes for my children to take notice. They offered to climb up and take care of it properly for me but again I state, I am terrified of heights and the thought of my children up there was not comforting. What to do? Then a thought struck me. What if I teach the children to parachute jump the way my dad had taught me years ago in an attempt to help me conquer this fear?

I asked if they wanted to learn. They responded with a resounding, "YES!" so we went to the back porch for practice. It was only about three feet high, so it was a safe height to learn from. After they mastered the art of tuck and roll, we moved to the front porch. It was about five feet high. Of course, by the time they were jumping off the carport, the whole neighborhood had joined in. What a sight it must have been to see my yard full of children jumping off my carport.

Each child held a fistful of gutter goo and pretended it was a grenade that they threw at the enemy as they parachuted into the field of battle. Shouts and cheers could be heard as the launched grenade hit a target. In a short time, my gutters were cleaned.

Several years later, our family was assisting in a building project for a sister church in a nearby city. We were all on different levels of this two-story building when my eldest son, who was on the roof, was struck by a runaway roll of tar paper. It knocked him off his feet, and he plummeted to the ground about twenty-five feet below. I heard the shouts and turned to watch in horror as he was nearing the ground. Then to my relief, he did the tuck and roll maneuver! My youngest child was on the rafters of the second story, and she lost her balance while turning to see what the commotion was and fell as well, also landing in the tuck and roll. They both jumped up and shouted, "IT WORKS!" The Pastor of the church looked at me in total disbelief and asked, "What do you teach your children?" I laughed and said, "Everything I can." With that being said, I encourage you to also teach your children everything you can. Especially, everything you can about God.

Takeaway: What we teach our children may seem insignificant in the moment, but it could have an eternal impact on their souls.

She Gave it Away

A lso regard not your stuff; for the good of all the land of Egypt is yours. *(Genesis 45:20)*

Our daughter's birthday was coming up. She was not a selfish child at all and rarely asked for anything. But there was a special ballerina Barbie that she desired. Though she would never ask for it, we knew. My husband and I did not have a lot of money for frivolous toys. This toy was expensive, at least for us. We discussed it, and we saved everything we could for three or four months to buy this toy for her for her birthday. The big day arrived. The party was great. Her friends were having fun. The presents were opened. And Daddy went in the back and pulled out the special gift we had saved for her. As she opened it, she was so ecstatic. She made the Barbie dance, and she shared it with her friends. They all had a great time, and one of her friends expressed a great interest in this doll of hers. By the time the party was over, my little angel gave that gift to her friend. How could she do this? I was feeling all kinds of emotions and was ready to jump in there and take that doll back. But my husband forbade me and said, "It's hers to give away." I didn't want to understand. I worked so hard! My husband and I both had scrimped and saved to get this for her. How could she just give it away? But in her eyes, it was just a toy. Her friend held far more value. She taught me in that moment of unselfishness that stuff is just stuff, but people are eternal. I need to put more value on what's truly important in life. I need to stop focusing on my stuff and focus on the true treasure I have. I have been given salvation full and free! I am forgiven and assured an eternity in Heaven! I need to share Jesus with my friends and family.

Takeaway: Giving his all was never unreasonable to Christ. He has put that much value on us.

Show Me How to Love Him

*B*ut when Jesus saw it, he was much displeased, and said unto them, Suffer the little children to come unto me, and forbid them not: for of such is the kingdom of God. (Mark 10:14)

Anyone who has taught a Sunday School class has met a child like this boy. He's the child who will not comply. If you ask him to be here, he goes there. As soon as you are not looking, he runs off. I ran a class of nearly sixty children, but I must constantly tend to or look for this one. AAAARG!!! I found myself praying he would not show up this week. Then I felt bad. He needed to learn of Jesus and his love for him as much as all the other children. Lord, what should I do? How can I love him? Well, the answer came one day when I thought I had actually lost this little man. He had run out the side exit towards the busy street that ran beside the church, and I panicked! I screeched an, "Excuse me!" to the class and ran after him and out the door. I grabbed him by the hand and sat him on the parking wall by the building. He was trying to shake my hand loose from his, but I would not let go.

With tears in my eyes, I told him, "You scared me. I thought I was going to lose you! I cannot bear the thought of losing you. I will not let go of your hand until I can give it to your mom. I love you so much. So, from now until then, you will have to be my left hand since you are now the owner of it. Deal?"

He looked at me with such a precious look of wonder, then smiled. "DEAL!" he shouted.

What a time we had in class. He smiled the whole time. The next week when he arrived for class, he held up his right hand and said, "Your other hand is here!" Oh, my heart was bursting with pride. He became a true treasure to the class and to me. He also received Jesus as his Savior within a few short weeks. It was not long after this chain of events that his mom asked for a meeting with me. She was the single mother of four boys, this young man being the eldest. She asked what I did to her boy. He was not the same boy he was a couple of months ago. So, I got the pleasure of sharing with her how God answered my prayer. That by refusing to let go of his hand, God showed him that he is valuable, loved, and too precious to lose. I also shared Jesus and his wonderful story of love with her, and she, too, is now a child of God. Thank you, Lord. By showing me how to love this precious boy, a whole family is now saved!

Takeaway: Every child is somebody's precious baby. Every child is loved by God.

The Good Gift

Therefore with joy shall ye draw water out of the wells of salvation. (Isaiah 12:3)

My first grandchild was turning 1 year old and was such a cute little thing. Lots of people showed up for her birthday party, mostly adults. The time finally came to open her presents. She was placed in the middle of the table and presents were handed to her one by one. So many gift bags! Inside each one of them was clothing. This little girl was less than thrilled about clothing, even to this day. But bag after bag had more clothing. We had to encourage her to keep opening the rest of her gifts and then two crisp $1.00 bills fell out of one of the gifts. She held them up in the air, one in each hand, and shouted, "WOOHOO WOOHOO!" We all laughed.

When she noticed that we were looking at her, she quickly tucked them underneath her leg and sat on them securely. Nobody was going to be allowed to take those from her. She continued opening her presents, but now with a cute little grin on her face. Periodically, she would check under her thigh to make sure those bills were still sitting there. She received plenty more clothing and finally a toy, but nothing was as precious to her as those two $1 bills. Clean-up time came, and her mommy went to pick her up, but not before she quickly reached down and grabbed her money. She refused to let anyone hold it for her.

God has given us a gift far more valuable than those two crisp $1.00 bills. Salvation. It is so precious and costly. But do we truly value it? I remember when I got saved. I came home so happy that I was rejoicing. I shared with everybody the new gift I had received. Some of them laughed at me while others made fun of me. But I wasn't letting go of this gift; I took it into my heart and kept it safe. Honestly, there's no way anybody could take this gift from me, but they did try to take away my joy. Salvation is so valuable; we should never be ashamed of it. We should never tuck it away safely. We should always display it and show off its value. It has a value far above rubies and is more precious than gold, and we need to make that known. Of all the gifts we could ever receive, salvation is one to shout about.

Takeaway: We should never forget how precious the gift of salvation is. Shout it out!

Reflection Day

This week we saw ways that children love. We tend to see them differently than God does. He loves them and desires that we love him in such a pure and complete manner. They love unconditionally. And they remember what they learn to be true. Can you write a few thoughts about how you see God? How you know beyond any doubt that he loves you. Remind yourself how you have seen Him in your life this week.

The Lord's Day

L ord, as we gather together in your house today, we pray that you will reveal yourself to us. Please help us to reach out to others you may bring into our lives today. And please, God, give unto us a youthful, unwavering faith.

Week 9

What's Missing?

The Missing Ingredient

*I*n the beginning was the Word, and the Word was with God, and the Word was God. The same was in the beginning with God. All things were made by him; and without him was not any thing made that was made. In him was life; and the life was the light of men. And the light shineth in darkness; and the darkness comprehended it not. (John 1:1-5)

My family loves sweet bread. Our household favorites are banana bread, zucchini bread, and pumpkin bread. I make them all the time. Sweet breads are simple and yet somewhat nutritious for a snack, or so I like to tell myself. I make them so often that I know the recipe by heart. In fact, my cookbook is losing pages from opening it to the same one so many times. One day, I was making pumpkin bread and whipped up a batch very quickly. As I pulled it from the oven for an afternoon snack, I noticed that it looked a bit pale. I couldn't quite figure out why. Was it because I used a homegrown pumpkin? Did I pull zucchini out of the freezer instead? WAIT! I forgot the pumpkin! The container of pumpkin was still sitting right there on the counter! Oh no! Everyone would be coming in at any moment to enjoy a snack, and I don't have anything but this bread that's missing the key ingredient! Only one thing to do... serve it as is and hope for the best. You know what? They didn't even notice. How can this be? Well, as I pondered this, I got to thinking about how my life was before

I found Christ. I cannot imagine my life without him now, but back then, I didn't even notice that He was missing from my life. He's the creator of the world. My creator. The one who loves me even though he knows me completely. He died to save me! He is the key ingredient to all life! How could I not know he was missing from my life? Just like my pumpkin bread that was missing the pumpkin, nobody noticed because they still tasted the cinnamon and spices and imagined the pumpkin was there. It was only after I told them that I had forgotten the pumpkin that they realized it had an incomplete flavor. Thank you, Lord, for having someone show me that you were missing from my life! My life is so much more enjoyable now that you are in the middle of it every day.

Takeaway: A life without Christ is flavorless and unfulfilling. Have you asked him to be your Savior?

The Missing Base

Thou believest that there is one God; thou doest well: the devils also believe, and tremble. (James 2:19)

All our children played Little League baseball. I sat on bleachers so much that I have a permanent impression of them on my.... ok, let's not talk about that! There was one Little League game, in particular, that sticks out in my memory. It was getting down to the wire. The child up to bat was not the strongest player on the team, but he had been practicing so very hard. Strike one! We all cheered him on. Strike two! "Next one is yours!" we shouted. At the next pitch... he swung and hit it deep into the outfield! He ran with all his might. First base, second base, third base, home! He slid in and stood there in a moment of victory. Then the catcher threw the ball to first base, and the umpire shouted, "OUT!" What?! How? He clearly ran all the bases and tagged home plate. What was going on? How could he call him out? Well, it turns out that as he rounded first base, he failed to step on it. Therefore, he never safely reached first base before the ball. So, he was indeed out. That one missed step cost him and the team the homer un.

Through the years, I have tried to share the gospel with people. I have found that many people sincerely believe in the existence of God. But may I say that one belief is not enough? Do you realize that Satan believes? Is he going to be in heaven at the end of his time? Of course not. He strives against God, refusing to acknowledge the deity and holiness that belong only to God. He strives to prove that he, too, can be like God. Therefore, believing alone cannot be enough. No, the Bible tells us that we must believe and receive the truth of the gospel. We must call upon Jesus in humble confession and repent, knowing that we need him to save us because we do not possess the power on our own to conquer our sin. The step we don't want to miss is confessing with our own mouth our need for Jesus, our Savior.

Takeaway: One missing base cost the team the homerun. Not asking Christ to save you from your sins could cost you an eternity.

Where's the Gas?

Submit yourselves therefore to God. Resist the devil, and he will flee from you.
(James 4:7)

Drifter. That's what he's known as. He just wanders around from place to place, finding work when he needs funding. That is how we met him. He wandered into our jobsite asking for work. We really needed help, so he was offered a day's wage and lunch. He far exceeded our expectations. He was an excellent worker. He offered to stay the rest of the week and help us finish the project. While he worked the week, we allowed him to camp in his tent in our backyard. He would share a ride with my husband each morning in our truck. On the way home from work that night, they stopped for gas. The next morning, our truck was gone! Yes, he stole our truck. He found a way into the house and took the keys from the hook and drove away! We prayed for our truck's safe return, but we also prayed for this young man and his need for salvation.

We were driving in our little car to the jobsite to try and finish the project when we saw it. Our truck was on the side of the road! There was no apparent damage. So why had he abandoned it? Well, this truck had two gas tanks. Yes, the tank my hubby had filled was the second tank, and the gauge was showing the tank was full. But he had not yet switched the tank over, just the gauge. So, our drifter was using up the gas in the first tank and ran out! One quick flip of the switch, and our truck was once again fully operational. Praise the Lord! As we continued up the road, we saw the drifter. He quickly ran into a local bar to hide. My hubby followed him in and asked for the keys back, which he gladly surrendered. See, his lack of knowledge of the basic functions of the truck caused him to fail. It's that way with Satan too. He is not all-knowing like God. In all his efforts to be like God, he still isn't. He isn't all powerful, he doesn't know all, he cannot see all, nor is he everywhere at one time. He is a pretender like our drifter. And because of this, we can resist him and have victory over the trials and struggles he sends our way.

Takeaway: Satan is not God. As God's child I have the power to resist him and be victorious.

Don't Miss the Opportunity

*P*reach the word; be instant in season, out of season; reprove, rebuke, exhort with all longsuffering and doctrine. (II Timothy 4:2)

It was a cool, misty morning. The sun was just beginning to peer over the horizon. One could almost hear the faint sound of a western theme song in the distance as the call rang out across the plains. Preacher! We need you! That's a call all too familiar to this man. He is committed to the cause of seeing souls won for Christ. Even retirement will not keep this dedicated Bible slinger from standing in the gap with a fellow preacher in need. I duly love this man! He's been shot down so many times, but he always rises and goes back into the thick of the fight. He literally has scars on his scars, but nothing stops him. He loves God so much; nothing will keep him down. Did you know that this is the call of every born-again believer? To be ready to give a testimony of the hope within you. You never know when the moment will strike. You could be on a simple trip to the store when the opportunity arises. Or, like this morning, you could be standing in the kitchen with one eye half open, making your coffee, when a text message buzzes in.

For my husband, preaching is his joy. He genuinely loves telling everyone about the Savior. Me? I would rather shrink away into a corner unnoticed. But the call is for all of us, so that includes me. So, how can a wall flower like me spread the word? Funny you should ask! Just the other day I was pumping gas when a total stranger came up to me and made a comment on all the packages I had in my jeep. I deliver mail for a living. Lately, it would be more accurate to say that I deliver Amazon and a little mail for a living. Anyway, he made a comment about my shopping addiction, and I laughed and joined in the conversation. Next thing you know, I invited him to church with a tract explaining the gospel message. I could not have done that if I was unprepared. I know what I believe. I study my Bible regularly to stay afresh on what I know to be true. I carry tracts to help in short moments or times when my brain is on vacation from my body. Be prepared! You and I must plan to be ready whenever God presents a moment. There are people out there who may not get another opportunity to hear the gospel. A missed opportunity rarely comes again. Please be ready to answer the ca ll.

Takeaway: Always be ready to share the hope inside you

Missing Her Heart

Judge not, that ye be not judged. For with what judgement ye judge, ye shall be judged: and with what measure ye mete, it shall be measured to you again. (Matthew 7:1-2)

A little girl lies on the couch in a fitful rest. Her fever is high, and she is delusional. Even asleep in the middle of the day, she is having nightmares. Everyone is praying for her. Her five-year-old big sister is worried as well. This isn't just her sister; she is also her best friend and playmate. She missed her fellowship and prayed her sister would feel better soon. As everyone busied themselves to make dinner, her big sister sat by her side. When her aunt came back to check on her, she found the big sister standing over her on the back of the couch, with a flashlight shining down on her.

"What are you doing?! Let her rest!" were the cries heard throughout the house.

Yet big sister gently replied, "I was making it a sunny day so she could have sweet dreams and feel better." Oh! My heart! How precious is that?

We judge others and their motives too quickly. Why is that? Is it really such a foreign concept to consider that every person is potentially trying to do their best in this crazy world? Everyone has dreams and goals. And everyone has different views and opinions. But that doesn't necessarily make them wrong just because they are different. I know that my ideas are unique to most people. But my ways work for me for the most part. I try to keep them in line with God and his standards. I also strive to learn more each day. It is my daily goal to please my Lord and my Savior. So, I must believe that you are doing your best as well. Let's let God judge. Afterall, He alone can see the thoughts and intentions of our hearts. And in the meantime, we can encourage others to strive for their best as well.

Takeaway: I should look for the good in others and encourage them through life.

Reflection Day

This week was a fun look at the missing things in life. Can you take a few moments to record some things you may have noticed missing in your life? How is God filling those voids for you?

The Lord's Day

Lord, we miss so many details in our daily lives. So many, we may never even be aware of them. Will you please help us and guide us to living a more fulfilled life in you? Help us see that you complete us in every way. Lord, please help us to share what we learn with others.

Week 10

It Will be Worth It

AWANA Night

Cast not away therefore your confidence, which hath great recompence of reward. For ye have need of patience, that, after ye have done the will of God, ye might receive the promise. For yet a little while, and he that shall come will come, and will not tarry. (Hebrews 10:35-37)

We used to take ten to twelve children with us every week to AWANA (Approved Workmen Are Not Ashamed) night. It's a Children's Bible Club hosted by our church. My hubby would take a few in the car with him and I would squish the rest into our crew cab pickup truck. The trip to church was always more enjoyable than the trip home. After the meeting, everyone was tired and hungry, which made for challenges. I found that if I promised to stop at the store for ice cream bars or a snack of choice, the children usually didn't fight about not having their own space in the seats. Since this was a weekly event, the main cashier on duty at our local store really thought I had ten children. I couldn't leave them alone in the truck for a variety of safety reasons.

These weekly stops also became very costly. Buying at least fifteen treats each week as well as gassing up both vehicles for a one and a half hour round trip added up! However, God always provided. We never lacked the needed funds for these adventures. The children were totally worth it! Sometimes as we go about our lives, we forget just how truly valuable the people in our lives are. Yes, it takes sacrifice and dedication to take a busload of children to church every week. They fight over silly things, complain that she is looking at me, or he is breathing my air. But if we do our best for God, he will always supply our needs and grace abundantly. We needed patience. We needed peace.

Many nights when I just wanted to get out and scream, God put a song in my heart and the whole group would join in singing with me. We were just as blessed by these weekly meetings and adventures as the children were. We must remember that children are learning from us. How we handle every aspect of life is being watched and one day will be mimicked. I hope and pray that I showed my children and all those others that they are important and that loving each other is job number one. I also pray that they learned that serving God is not only our duty, but it is our utmost joy and totally worth the struggles.

Takeaway: Serving God is not convenient, but it is worth the sacrifice and brings us joy.

Daddy is Great

A nd he answered and said unto them, my mother and my brethren are these which hear the word of God, and do it. (Luke 8:21)

One of my favorite sports is watching children play with their daddy. What? You've never heard of it? It's a great activity. My kids used to tackle their dad as soon as he got home from work each night. He would gently toss them to and fro across the living room, mostly onto the couch, I am surprised that it held up as well as it did under such action. There would be pillows flying in all directions! The kids would squeal and run back repeatedly for more of the same. This mountain of a man would have every child on him all at once, hanging off his leg, his arm, even his neck at the same time. They loved their daddy and needed to have those bonding moments with him each day. Even now that they are grown, they still need time with their daddy. Oh, not in a physical wrestling match so much as just in time with him. Doing whatever or nothing. Just time together.

This is such a beautiful picture of our relationship with our Heavenly Father. We need our moments with him as well if we are to feel complete and bonded with Him. Most of us have no problem sharing our hearts and lives with him in prayer. But it's that time spent with him in devotion and studying his word when he shares with us. Occasionally, we just need time sitting on the porch, watching the grass grow and reflecting in a prayerful attitude. No relationship works well if there are not at least two people putting into it. It takes effort on each side to make it work. God is faithful. He shows up each and every day. We need to show up and put into the relationship as well.

Takeaway: I must devote a few minutes each day to letting God communicate with me. I must learn to listen to him; he listens to me all the time.

No Longer in Egypt

Therefore shall ye keep my commandments, and do them: I am the LORD. Neither shall ye profane my holy name; but I will be hallowed among the children of Israel: I am the LORD which hallow you, That brought you out of the land of Egypt, to be your God: I am the LORD. (Leviticus 22:31-33)

The house we live in is so very old. It was built in 1907. Oh, if walls could talk, right? I know a little bit of its history. At least a little about the owners that lived here before us. The police in our town tell a tale as well that this house was used as a drug house. There was a group of people partying in the house that shared the same needle for their drugs, and that needle was infected with a flesh-eating bacterium. Eight of the people in that party died while others suffered terribly. There were bloodstains on the carpet and on the walls. There were also spatters of blood on the ceilings. We were able to scrub away most of it and paint over the stains. But there's one particular stain on the ceiling in one of the rooms. It's a spatter that spreads across a good section. No matter what we do, that spatter keeps resurfacing. How many kinds of stain blockers can we use? How many layers of paint? It is only a matter of time, until the spatter is back again. Those of us who suffer from PTSD can understand this. It doesn't matter how much counselling we go through or how many years have passed, something can still trigger us back into that terrible nightmare that we suffered.

I wonder if this is how the children of Israel felt. They were delivered from Egypt, out of slavery. They were given promises of a bright, healthy and prosperous future. Yet, they keep turning back to their idols, extending their journey for many years. They eventually even asked God to give them a king to govern over them. Was it because, even though they were out of Egypt, Egypt was not out of them? Some of them were born into slavery, others had lived in slavery most of their life. Was the trauma still part of who they were? At times, it's hard to let go of our past and live in the victory God has gifted us with. It's even harder for those of us who have been beaten down for so long to see ourselves as anything special. But we are children of the king! That makes us princes and princesses! Lord, help us leave our Egypt behind and live in our promised land.

Takeaway: I no longer live in my past. I am a testament to God's grace and mercy. Right here! Right now! I don't need to dwell on yesterday, nor make it part of today.

Twin Markets

Behold, how good and how pleasant it is for brethren to dwell together in unity! (Psalm 133:1)

There are two mini markets near my home. One of them is thriving and business is booming. People are in and out all the time. Yet I hardly see a car show up at the other one. What's the difference? They both look pretty much the same. They have the same merchandise and the same pricing. So why is one busy and the other empty? Could it be the atmosphere presented inside the store? When you enter the busy store, you are greeted by a smiling clerk behind the counter who invites you to see what's on special that day. He has a vibrant personality and offers to help you if you need anything. In contrast, once you step into the empty store, the clerk watches your every move. He is staring with a cold glare as if you may steal something if he isn't vigilant in watching you place each item back in its proper place. If you ask for help to find an item, he gets irritated and flays his arms around violently in the direction of what you seek. Our churches are the same way.

When a visitor enters our doors, do we invite them in and show them around? Do we introduce them to people and the Pastor? Do we invite them to future events coming up that might interest them? Do we show them Jesus? In my little town, there are so many churches to choose from. Some are large, some small and quaint. But what is dwelling inside the hearts of the believers is where we find the heartbeat of our church. It's also where we find the opportunity to let the love of Jesus shine through. What is the heart of your church like? People are looking for God. They want to be accepted. Let's take the first step and show them kindness and welcome them at the doors of the church. Create an atmosphere of love.

Takeaway: People will not stay where they don't feel welcomed

Mall Stories

But the LORD said unto Samuel, Look not on his countenance, or on the height of his stature; because I have refused him: for the LORD seeth not as man seeth; for man looketh on the outward appearance, but the LORD looketh on the heart. (I Samuel 16:7)

I sat in the mall today. Just watching people. No, I'm not a crazy stalker. I was looking for a story, or maybe just some basic ideas. I saw a group of boys come in with a "gangster" attitude, manner, and dress. I could stereotype them and tell all kinds of wild tales about them. But honestly, what I saw today was just a group of boys that genuinely understood each other. They are friends, true friends. And they may have mischief in their hearts, but I don't really know. Today I just saw a group of boys having fun together and enjoying each other's company.

Then I saw a family over on my left. The baby would not quit crying. Just a young toddler, probably bored with shopping. It has to be hard on such a young child to go to the mall and see so many fantastic and wonderful things and not be able to touch anything. To not be allowed to leave the safety of the stroller. Mom and Dad are touching everything. Why can't he? He's crying, "Take me home where I can touch something! That's all I want right now! I just want to play. But for now, I'll just yell!" Yes, I'm just making all this up. I don't know what's going on inside these people. I cannot see their true intentions. I definitely cannot see into their hearts. And you know, it really doesn't matter what I think about these people at all. It only matters what God thinks.

As we go about our lives, we should only worry about what God thinks of us. Yes, everywhere we go people are watching. They may even be judging us. They could be talking about us. But God is the one we need to please each and every day. He is our only true judge. We should be most concerned about what the Lord thinks and make sure that we measure up to His standards. Are we keeping our testimony clean? According to the Bible, we should make an honest effort to present ourselves holy and undefiled. Every day is a new opportunity; we should try to present ourselves as if the Lord himself was standing right beside us watching, listening, and trusting us to represent him well. We should at least try

.

Takeaway: People are important, but they are not who I am supposed to strive to please. God is. If I please him, I will probably be at peace with the people in my life too.

Reflection Day

People! We have talked about people a lot lately. Can you think of ways that God has used people to speak to you this week? Journal the ways they impacted you.

The Lord's Day

Heavenly Father, as we go to church this morning, please give us insight into the needs around us. Help us be welcome and warm to any visitors you see fit to bring our way. Please also help us remember that you are the one we strive to please each and every day. That it's your praise we truly seek. Forgive us for our weaknesses. Could you please wipe away any lingering hurt from past offenses and help us to truly forgive, so we can see others through YOUR eyes?

Week 11

Creating the Right Environment

The Story

*F*or I am not ashamed of the gospel of Christ: for it is the power of God unto salvation to every one that believeth; to the Jew first, and also to the Greek. *(Romans 1:16)*

All day long, there were children in and out of my house. Many days I can recall the kids running in and shouting, "You will never guess what just happened!" One particular day, I recall my youngest came running out of the woods screaming, "There's a bear!" She was pointing in the direction and telling me the boys were still there. So, I go running to get the boys to safety.

Along the way, my young son comes out and says, "The bear came into the fort! It came right at me!" Now I'm running faster! And as I approach the fort, fearing what I might find, my eldest son and his friend come out. They are excited and both start telling me about the bear as well. To the smaller boy, it was a big black bear. To my tall son, it was a medium brown bear. But then my son adds to the story and tells me how the bear took hold of his hand to take some French fries from him. They all saw the account from their own perspective and because of this, they all told me the story a bit differently. Different people have different perspectives.

The same is true of the gospel and the four authors: Matthew, Mark, Luke, and John. Each of them gives an account of the events of Christ's life. Many times, they speak of the same events. Yet they vary in detail. Matthew portrays Christ as the Messiah telling of his coming Kingdom. Mark details him as a humble servant expressing love for those he came to serve. While Luke, the physician, depicts Christ as God in the flesh, the man who lived a sinless life in perfect submission to his Father's will. John focuses on the divinity and majesty of Christ and his great love for the entire world. Since all four writers came from different lifestyles, communities, families, and different economic backgrounds, they have different views of the world, and they write to different audiences. They shared with us the events as they saw them, so that we could have a chance to know and love Jesus as they did. In turn, each of us has met Christ in a unique way. We each have a unique perspective of how our lives were impacted by the love of Christ. The gospel of Christ is too fantastic to keep to ourselves. It must be shared.

Takeaway: You don't need to have someone tell you the perfect way to share the gospel with others. Tell about it from your own heart. Tell how Christ has impacted you.

Not in the Winter

Keep thy heart with all diligence; for out of it are the issues of life.
(Proverbs 4:23)

Winter brings change to our lives. We change toys by putting away bikes and skateboards and pulling out the tubes and sleds. We change our wardrobe and store the swimwear and sandals to trade up for the more practical coats and boots.

I never let my kids climb the trees in the winter. They always thought it was because it's slippery in wintertime, but I was trying to protect the trees. The trees are in such a deep state of hibernation at that time that they are extremely fragile. Their limbs are deprived of many of the nutrients they need for strength. They are dry and brittle. In this delicate state of survival, it would not take much to damage them beyond the recovery that springtime brings.

The Bible tells us to guard our hearts. It is imperative that we protect it at all costs. There are several input sources to our spiritual heart. Our eyes, our ears, our noses, our hands, and our feet to start with. I love the smell of fresh baked bread, the view of the mountain as the sun is rising in the morning, the sound of children singing songs and the touch of their hugs. All these senses bring warm and fuzzy feelings to my soul. My lips speak well of them.

On the contrary, if I fill my senses with evil sights, sounds, and touches, I will have more of the same flowing out of my mouth. I have a coworker who is always talking with such foul language. Try as I might to ignore him, I leave his presence with those wretched words stuck in my head. It takes conscious effort to purge them from my thoughts. The things we allow ourselves to be exposed to become part of our character. We must be careful to guard our hearts from the influence of evil. What we absorb from exposure will be reflected in how we behave and react when trials come our way. Like the trees in wintertime, when we are under the pressure of a fiery trial, we could irreparably crack. If we are careful to protect ourselves during the good times, we are less likely to break in the hard times.

Takeaway: I need to carefully choose what I allow myself to be exposed to. It has an effect on me whether I realize it or not.

Beautiful as I Am

*T*hine eyes did see my substance, yet being unperfect; and in thy book all my members were written, which in continuance were fashioned, when as yet there was none of them. How precious also are thy thoughts unto me, O God! How great is the sum of them! If I should count them, they are more in number than the sand: when I awake, I am still with thee. (Psalm 139:16-18)

Us women are always comparing ourselves to each other. It's a silly practice yet we do it. The Bible often tells us to consider nature, so, let's look at dogs today. There are so many different dogs, and each of them is uniquely created and special. German shepherds bark aggressively and fiercely while Saint Bernards simply woofs. Beagles let out big bellowing sounds that seem like they will run out of air before it ever stops. The tiny Yorkies and Chihuahuas will yip, yip, yip. Though they all are dogs, they all have different natures. That's why they bark differently and behave differently. A cattle dog will herd everything into an area where he thinks it belongs, including children. While other dogs are severely territorial and they chase everything away, even barking at their owners at times. They have different places in their doggy society. We understand that about animals. We know that they behave differently, and we accept that. However, when it comes to ourselves, we constantly compare. If only I had hair like hers.

If only I could sing like that. I wish I could play piano like her. She's so graceful, and I'm so, so, me. Why do we torture ourselves like that?

We are perfect just the way we are. We are created in the image of God for a special purpose. It's not the same purpose as the other lady of course, so why are we trying to be like her? We should be who we are created to be. You and I are beautiful! Each in our own way. If you be the best you can be, and I be the best I can be... others can just be happy for us. Wouldn't that be something?

Takeaway: I will never be anything but me. Why torture myself trying to be something I was never meant to be? Thank you, Lord, for creating me to be who you want me to be. Help me to be the best I can be. Help me to show others that you know what you are doing in making each of us unique and special.

Press Toward the Mark

Brethren, I count not myself to have apprehended: but this one thing I do, forgetting those things which are behind, and reaching forth unto those things which are before, I press toward the mark for the high calling of God in Christ Jesus. (Philippians 3:13-14)

Ever notice how many coaches there are on a baseball team? There's the pitching coach, the first base coach, the third base coach, and let's not forget the head coach and the assistant coach. And that's just little league baseball! There might be more for professional ball teams. At our Little League games, I often witnessed that as a batter would hit the ball and run towards first base, the only thing the batter was focused on was running as fast as he could to that base. As he neared the base, the first base coach would instruct him to stay or continue running to second base. It was at second base where the runner focused on instruction from the third base coach who would guide him to home plate. Why did he need these coaches? Couldn't he just look around for himself and make the decision? Well, these coaches had a better view of where the ball was. They could see more clearly what action was taking place in the field. For the batter to run faster, he needed to focus on the pathway he was running and the obstacles in that path. The coaches were there to assist and instruct him so he could reach his goal safely.

Satan has set up snares and pitfalls in our pathway of life. He is truly trying to knock us out of the game. Fortunately, Jesus has promised to be there every step of the way. Guiding, protecting, and assisting us as we need. Coaching us. He sees exactly what is going on and can lead us through each step if we listen to his instruction. If we keep our eyes on the goal and on our Savior, we are assured victory.

Takeaway: We cannot be good Christians without Christ. He sees the enemy far better than we can.

Bad Directions

My sheep hear my voice, and I know them, and they follow me: And I give unto them eternal life; and they shall never perish, neither shall any man pluck them out of my hand. (John 10:27-28)

Have you ever gotten lost? Way back before GPS, my sister and I would go for drives and just drive. Then we would try to find our way back home. It was always an adventure. There were times when we really didn't know where we were and had to stop to get directions. One time, we left Indianapolis where we lived and started heading east. We had never been that way before. It wasn't long before we were in Ohio. The signs were reading: Cincinnati 20 miles. Oops! Maybe we were having a little too much fun and forgot to watch the time. We stopped for a bite to eat before heading back. But we didn't pay attention to the roads as we exited the highway either. We just followed the signs to the restaurant. Of course, the signs only led one way. They weren't there to guide us back. Yep, we were lost. The further we went, the worse it got. No cell phone, no map, nothing to help us. To make matters worse, it was beginning to get dark too. We stopped and asked for directions at a gas station. The clerk must have thought that it would be a great game to send us the wrong way. He did a good job! We got even further from our destination. Well, we finally decided to stop and ask a farmer who was out tending his cows for help. Yes, we were that far from civilization. He drew us a map on some paper we had in the car and sent us on our way back home. It was near bedtime by the time we returned and the trouble we were in is a story for another day. But we were safe.

The point I want to share is this: The clerk gave us bad directions. He did it purposely to entertain himself. He had no concern for the two young ladies he put in danger. The farmer, on the other hand, was willing to lead us to the highway but we convinced him to draw a map instead. He would have sacrificed his supper and time to help us. Does this sound similar to Satan and Christ? Satan loves to mislead us and get us far from where we ought to be. He finds great joy in deceiving us while Christ searches for us when we go astray. He gave us the Bible, accessory prayer, and so much more including his own life to help us. He would never lead us wrong. Be very careful who you are listening to.

Takeaway: If you are following Jesus, you will never be lost. He would never lead you in the wrong direction.

Reflection Day

I t is really hard to stay positive in a negative world. So many pressures are placed upon us to be perfect. How has God reassured you this week?

The Lord's Day

Lord, we know that you created each of us with unique features and individual quirky personalities for a reason. We pray that you help us be the best we can be and to use the talents you gave us for your glory. Help us be confident in who we are created to be. And Lord, please protect us from the evil ones who try to bring us down or lead us astray. We trust you for strength and praise you for it.

Week 12

The Right Environment

50/50

*And they twain shall be on flesh: so then they are no more twain, but one flesh.
(Mark 10:8)*

I was always told that marriage was a 50/50 relationship. Meaning that each partner does their half of the work to keep the marriage strong and thriving. I disagree. Let's do the math. Yes, if we add 50+50, we get 100. But that's the wrong equation when it comes to marriage. God says that when a couple joins in wedlock, they are no longer two but one. So, if 2=1, then 50+50=100/2, which still equals fifty. In other words, you cannot make a half-hearted effort and get your best result. Each person needs to give their whole self to make a marriage work. I'm not negating the fact that there are times when we cannot always give 100%, like when we are sick, or right after the birth of a baby. But during those down times, we can still express love and do our best to value our spouse.

So, as in the marriage equation, it is still 100% of what we are capable of in the moment of need. Marriages cannot survive if only one person is putting forth all the effort. The marriage began because two people were giving it all they had to impress and support each other. Why does that need to stop? It shouldn't. I have been married forever! Ha ha! It has been over forty years now, and my hubby and I still hold hands. We still say I love you before we go to bed each night. Yes, even if we are having a tiff over something. If you think about it, ten years from now, will what you are fighting over matter? The only thing I really would fight with him about are the children because, that will matter in the future. But just because I have a different view doesn't mean his opinion is wrong either. That's not easy to see in the heat of the moment. But in giving my 100%, I must consider his heart and his view in every matter as well. I must remind myself that he loves our children too and wants what is best for them. I must respect him at all costs, just like when we were dating, and I would submit my will to his to win his heart. I will also do it at times to keep his heart. And he will do it for me as well.

Two-way communication is key. And even more valuable than that is prayer. A couple that prays together, stays together. It's in the moments of holding each other in prayer that we see each other's truest heart. I hear him pour words out to God that he doesn't tell me face to face. I don't know why, maybe because children can talk to their father easier. Afterall, isn't that who God is? Our Heavenly Father. Jesus gave his all for both of us. It is not unreasonable for me to put forth my best effort.

Takeaway: I must not slack in my relationship with my spouse. He is half of who I am in the eyes of God. I am going to help him succeed and grow in faith. I will use my 100% to help him become the man he dreams of being and the man I know he can be.

The Pin Cushion

A prudent man foreseeth the evil, and hideth himself: but the simple pass on, and are punished. By humility and fear of the LORD are riches, and honour, and life. Thorns and snares are in the way of the froward: he that doth keep his soul shall be far from them. Train up a child in the way he should go: and when he is old, he will not depart from it. (Proverbs 22:3-6)

I used to make all our clothing. It was so much cheaper. This was a way that we could all wear stylish clothing without the high cost. It was also a way to make a little money from home. To do this, I had to spend time shopping at the fabric store sales for deals. That's where the problem was. My young children would get bored very quickly. There was a day that one of the children decided to see how many pins could be found on the floor. As soon as a pin was found, it was safely tucked into the front pocket of their jeans. When the time came to go home, we were getting seated in the car, but this child found it very difficult to sit down and get buckled into the car seat. I asked the child, "What's wrong?" No answer. It was a very short investigation as the protruding pocket became evident and the pain it was causing was obvious.

This is one of those teaching moments that usually gets passed over. There really was no expense here. Straight pins at that time cost about twenty-five cents for a package of 250. There were about 100+ in this pocket. But at four years old, this was stealing and a start to deception on a new level. I wanted to get home. This was inconvenient! But I made the decision to teach my toddler not to steal. I unpacked the children from the car and marched my youngster up to the manager and asked for a minute. Then I had my child show her what was stolen.

Lord, thank you for a very wise and understanding manager! She looked and gasped the sincerest gasp of horror. "Never, in all my days, has anyone ever stolen so much from me before!" she said. Tears began flowing from my toddler and myself.

She explained that she needed a minute to think about what to do and asked the youngster to sit down by the counter. I imagine that my little one sat there fearing the police and a future in jail. After a few moments that felt like an eternity, she said she thought I was a good momma and that I could be trusted to teach my children not to steal in the future and released my child back to my arms. We were finally on our way home. As hard as this seems, prison would be harder. We must teach our children right and wrong so they can choose wisely in the future. They must know there are consequences to sin and wrongdoing. There is a penalty that lasts for all eternity, and we must prepare them for that choice when they face it. There will come a day when they need to choose for themselves to ask Jesus to save them or pass on the gift of God. I pray they choose Jesus.

Takeaway: It is better to teach our children young about the consequences of wrongdoing. So they are better equipped to make wise choices when they are grown.

Put God First

He also that received seed among the thorns is he that heareth the word; and the care of this world, and the deceitfulness of riches, choke the word, and he becometh unfruitful. (Matthew 13:22)

As a whole, parents try really hard to teach their children. They do the best they know how to do. That's why God gave us a church family. We encourage and strengthen each other. Together, we can teach our children more than the world and give them a greater purpose. I see all too often that we let other things take the place of going to church. Yes, I believe family time is important; however, if we allow anything to stand in the way of going to church, before you know it, they're doing these things more often. Church service and God then take a back seat to activities. When will dedication to God be important? Will they serve God as adults if it's not a priority now while they're under our tutelage? In the Parable of the Sower and the seed, there's a section where the Lord mentions people who live in the weeds. He is referring to lost people in this passage, but if we apply it to born-again believers, here's what I see: They never reach the potential God has for them because they are choked by their surroundings, or in other words, the cares of the world take over. The fishing trip, the football game, the camping trip, the part-time job, whatever it is, kept them from growing spiritually. He calls them unfruitful, or unprofitable, someone he will never get his investment back from. And think about it, he invested greatly in each of us. Unless they are replanted in a healthier environment, they will not be productive for God. Let's not let that happen to our children. Take them to church before they spiritually die. Plant them in good soil. Watch them grow in the light of God's word. Son-light is good for all of us.

Takeaway: God created each of us and gave us gifts and abilities to fulfill a purpose. Don't let the world choke you or your children out spiritually and put all that potential to waste.

Pass the Plate

*E*very man according as he purposeth in his heart, so let him give; not grudgingly, or of necessity: for God loveth a cheerful giver.(... Now he that ministereth seed to the sower both minister bread for your food, and multiply your seed sown, and increase the fruits of your righteousness;) Being enriched in every thing to all bountifulness, which causeth through us thanksgiving to God. (II Corinthians 9:7&10-11)

I had a burst of pride this morning in church as I watched the children in the pew in front of me turn to their mommy and asked for an offering. See, every week as the offering is taken, I give the children around me money to put in. Children love to give. It's more accurate to say that they take great pride in giving. It does my heart good to see the influence of my small gestures on the younger generation. In little steps like this, the seed of giving has been planted in their tender hearts. They are the epitome of the verse that says to give with joy and not begrudgingly. As the offering plate nears them, they jump up and wave their gift in the air so it will not be missed. God forbid they are passed over! They will chase the usher down or stand there crying until their small gift is received.

Let's take this a step farther by showing them to do acts of kindness for elderly brothers and sisters in the church. Now the seed of service is planted in them. They can carry items for the sweet lady with a walker. Watch their faces light up with complete joy as she bends down to say softly, "Thank you, you are such a good helper." I have witnessed time and time again as they search for her at the start of each service to help her. If she has nothing to carry, they will hold a door open for her to walk through. She becomes their personal mission field. As they grow, they receive a sense of self-worth from these gestures of kindness, they will begin to do them on their own without prodding, without guidance. Their friends will also join in and others in the congregation are equally blessed by these fine young servants of God. None of us are promised tomorrow. We must teach the younger generation today while there is still time. They are the future of our church.

Takeaway: Giving to God goes way beyond monetary gifts. He wants us to give ourselves as well. Give the insight of your heart to a child and watch it grow into something beautiful.

Baby Food

A *nd I, brethren, could not speak unto you as unto spiritual, but as unto carnal, even as unto babes in Christ. I have fed you with milk, and not with meat: for hitherto ye were not able to bear it, neither yet now are ye able. (I Corinthians 3:1-2)*

It's no secret that some of us get really offended by being called a baby. That phrase implies that we are not capable of handling the reality we are facing. Yet God has called us that several times. He calls us newborn babes, little children, and more. Today's passage of Scripture tells the people they are so immature that they cannot even handle hearing the Word of God read to them. Because of this, Paul says he is feeding them milk instead of meat. Wow! It reminds me of when my children were tiny. They would sit in the highchair by the table and look at the food spread before them. Then I would bring them their plate. It didn't look like the grand display on the table so they would get upset and insist that they eat what I have on my plate. The problem was that they didn't have teeth. How were they going to be able to properly chew the food so they wouldn't choke on it? So, I would take a portion of my food onto their plate and shred it to bits for them so they could eat it. They would then gladly receive it.

The Bible is our spiritual food. It is given to us so we can learn of God and grow to our full potential in his will. But some of us are not good at listening and applying what we hear. We hear the word and get offended that anyone could suggest there is a problem with our behavior. 'Who says it's wrong?!' is the attitude. So, in the Scripture today, Paul addresses this by saying, "You are too immature or carnal to hear the whole truth, so I am breaking down to a simpler form for you. That way, you won't choke and die spiritually on what I'm about to say." Oh, dear friend, don't let this be true of you.

I know I get offended when someone tells me I am wrong. I try not to respond in the moment, but instead say something like, "Thank you for that insight, I was unaware I was doing that." It is best to take the words they speak to me and pray over them. I should take into consideration that it is not easy to approach someone with a fault. God is always faithful. He reveals to us the answers we seek if we come to him in prayer. Many times, I have found that I was wrong as my friend stated to me. To grow up in Christ, we must be willing to take correction to heart and be willing to change accordingly.

Takeaway: If we are honest with ourselves, each of us has areas of our life that need improvement. I pray I will never get to a point where I will not receive instruction. I want to be the best I can be for Christ.

Day of Reflection

There are so many areas to consider while creating the right environment. From our marriage to our children and those we encounter in our daily activities and more. Take a few moments to record any ideas God has given you this week. How can you make your home a positive environment for all who live there? What about your church, your jobsite, or anywhere else he has laid on your heart? Is he prodding you to make a change? Take note and grow.

The Lord's Day

Lord, as we begin a new day in your house, worshipping you, I pray you will enlighten us and help us be receptive to whatever you have to say. Help us see that correction and instruction are beneficial in nature, not critical. Lord, help us focus on our own improvement and not our neighbors or our spouses. I am the only one I can change or control, so help me grow in that truth. Thank you for always investing in me.

Week 13

It's the Little Things

Jesus Loves Little Ones

Then there were brought to him little children, that he should put his hands on them, and pray: and the disciples rebuked them. But Jesus said, Suffer little children, and forbid them not, to come unto me: for of such is the kingdom of heaven. And he laid his hands on them, and departed thence. (Matthew 19:13-15)

The first ministry our Pastor placed us in was the bus ministry. We were required to visit the children on our route each week and keep general reports for the Pastor, so he was able to effectively pray for them as well. Since we were newbies, we were given the route in the hard part of town. Within no time at all, our bus was full to overflowing. As my hubby drove, I would sing and play games with the children. They were given candy on the way home as they exited the bus. But they were also given hugs if they reached out for one. Then a little girl on our bus invited a neighbor girl to join us. She was only about five years old. She wore a heavy coat every day, even in the heat of summer. Her hair was always matted, and she smelled like she had never had a bath. The first few rides she took with us, she just sat quietly in her seat and watched as the beach ball we were playing with bounced around. She saw each of the children jump up to get off the bus and give me hugs. She had the cutest smile and the most infectious laugh. Then one day, we stopped to pick her up and it happened! As she came onto the bus, she ran straight to me and gave me a sweet hug! Then she sat in the seat with me! This became the new normal for her. No matter which seat I was in that day, she sat right there with me. She would hold my hand through church and snuggle into my lap quite often. I was asked many times by other ladies in the church how I could do this since she smelled so very bad, and her smell would rub off on my clothing as well. But honestly, how could I refuse her? She was a precious little girl who only needed love and acceptance. Jesus would never turn a child seeking his affection away. Children followed him everywhere he went. I think the disciples grew weary of them and tried turning them away so they could rest. But Jesus reprimanded them and said to let the children come. I loved this little girl; she was a precious jewel to me each week. My clothing washed out just fine and so did my hands. But I don't think she ever washed my love off her. I think it sank in clear to her bones and her heart. I was Jesus to her until she met him for herself.

Takeaway: You can never go wrong by loving children. They are a sample of what the kingdom of heaven is made of.

A Cup of Coffee

Then shall the righteous answer him, saying, Lord, when saw we thee an hungred, and fed thee? Or thirsty, and gave thee drink? And the King shall answer and say unto them, Verily I say unto you, Inasmuch as ye have done it unto one of the least of these my brethren, ye have done it unto me. (Matthew 25:37&40)

The wedding was over, and the next day had dawned. We were too poor for a honeymoon, so we had a staycation. My new husband insisted we had to do something for memory's sake, so we pondered on it a while and decided to go to Pizza Hut. That's pretty memorable. How many people can say they went to Pizza Hut for their honeymoon? As the waiter served our pizza, I noticed a young woman sitting at the table adjacent to ours. She had been there longer than us but there was nothing on her table. Not even a drink. I asked the waiter if she had been helped, to which he nodded yes. She looked so sad. I told my hubby. He went over and invited her to share with us. I was standing with him and then sat down beside her and assured her that we would very much like for her to at least take some of our food. She said she would think about it.

We returned to our table and a few minutes later she came over and asked if we were for real. "Yes," we both replied. So, she took a piece and said thank you, then asked for a cup of coffee, which the waiter quickly brought. Well, it turns out that our new friend was contemplating suicide that afternoon.

She was convinced that nobody in the world cared about her at all. Then we came along and noticed her need for companionship. Seriously? A little thing like a cup of coffee and a slice of pizza gave her enough self-worth to stop the suicidal thoughts? In this case, yes. She was begging God to show her that her life mattered, and someone walked over and asked her to join them for their honeymoon dinner. That was pretty special to her even though it was a small thing to us.

In the Bible (Mark 5: 25-34) there is a story of a woman who had suffered twelve years with an issue of blood. She had spent all her money, seen every physician she could, and been through many treatments, but she wasn't any better. In fact, she was worse. In desperation, she sought out Jesus. When she reached out and touched Jesus's garment, she was instantly healed. Jesus asked who touched him, and she revealed herself to him. The disciples, who were with Jesus, thought nothing of someone touching him, after all, they were in a crowd. But to her, it was everything. Her life was changed from that moment on. I would love to think that our new friend never again thought of suicide. I truthfully don't know. But I do know that she was very grateful for a few minutes of our time in conversation and a cup of coffee shared.

Takeaway: Little things mean a lot sometimes. Don't neglect to reach out, even in small ways. It could change someone's life forever.

Music Talks

Rejoice in the LORD, O ye righteous: for praise is comely for the upright. Praise the LORD with harp: sing unto him with the psaltery and an instrument of ten strings. Sing unto him a new song; play skilfully with a loud noise. (Psalm 33:1-3)

Music is a universal language. Ever heard that before? It's true. Everywhere you go in this world, you will hear music. It takes on different forms, but it's there, just like love. I find it amazing how therapeutic it can be. Ever notice how even animals enjoy listening to and sometimes dancing to music? My piano is in my sunroom and above one of the windows is a wire leading into the house. I sit there playing my heart out to the Lord and look up and there will be a tiny swallow perched on that wire. She is singing her heart out while I play. Her favorite tunes to tweet along with are Victory in Jesus and Somebody Loves Me. It doesn't take long, and there will be several little birdies on the line bobbing and singing along their praises to God, making a joyful noise to their Creator.

It's been proven that even plants enjoy music. I recently received an African violet as a prize at a church event. Within two days, my poor violet plant looked near to death. I have never been very skilled with those tender plants. The thought came to me to put it on my piano. It would get 180° of sunlight exposure and maybe the music each day would affect it too. I placed it there and played one hymn and took off to work. Upon my return, I noticed that it was standing tall and strong and as beautiful as ever! And today, a week later, it has new blooms! I'm so thrilled! God talks of music often in his word, the Bible. King David was a very skilled musician. He played while in the field with his sheep. He was also asked many times to play for King Saul to soothe his anxiety.

We are so blessed to have a God that loves us so much that he bestows upon us tiny treasures to enlighten our lives. He has surrounded us with a multitude of little things like music to saturate our days and make life more enjoyable. We have music all around us most of the day and don't even realize it. Take time to notice how it blesses your heart and then take a moment to thank God for it.

Takeaway: Lord, thank you so much for all the little ways you bless and encourage us. Music is just one of the many ways you enrich our lives. Again, thank you!

More Belly

For where envying and strife is, there is confusion and every evil work. But the wisdom that is from above is first pure, then peaceable, gentle, and easy to be entreated, full of mercy and good fruits, without partiality, and without hypocrisy. And the fruit of the righteous is sown in peace of them that make peace.   (James 3:16-18)

"I'm off to the gym. I need to work on my Mo-belly," that is what I heard as my son was taking off to the gym. I thought at first that he was making fun of me. I have put on a bit of weight lately. Yes, the extra servings of my favorite candy-coated chocolates are affecting my belly. And honestly, I'm a bit sensitive to that fact. I know I'm getting fat, but nobody else needs to know it. God forbid they should say it! Well, I immediately repeated what I heard him say but in a sarcastic tone, "Yea, you really need to work on that Mo-belly." He turned and laughed and said slowly and distinctly, "Mobility," then began stretching his shoulder that he recently had corrective surgery on. OH! Silly me. I misunderstood him and was hurt by what I thought I heard. How sad it could have been if I didn't listen to his explanation of what he meant for me to hear. I could have walked around with a chip on my shoulder all day. It might have affected how I faced him tomorrow or the next day.

An offense is hard to put aside at times. God warns us about letting strife have a place in the church. I am an easy target since I am the Pastor's wife. And let's face it, I am anything but the perfect lady. I have overheard and been greatly hurt by things that were said. Sadly, there have been times when each of us has experienced this. We must be careful not to let it take root in our heart and cause bitterness. This kind of bitterness and anger only causes trouble. We could easily find ourselves wanting this person to hurt the way they hurt us. Or wanting to say things to get people to respect them less. But it only has the opposite effect. This is not how God wants us to handle issues that arise between us. If we look at people the way God may see them, we are less likely to take offense to the petty things that come our way. Forgiveness is the first thing on God's heart. He loved all of us that much. We need to work harder to let it go and focus on the real issues. We are all one family in Christ. Let's communicate love to each other better.

Takeaway: Sometimes, we misunderstand each other. Strife between believers is never good. Let's practice better communication and forgiveness.

Stones of Remembrance

A nd he spake unto the children of Israel, saying, When your children shall ask their fathers in time to come, saying, What mean these stones? Then ye shall let your children know, saying, Israel came over this Jordan on dry land. For the LORD your God dried up the waters of Jordan from before you, until ye were passed over, as the LORD your God did to the Red sea, which dried up from before us, until we were gone over: That all the people of the earth might know the hand of the LORD, that it is mighty: that ye might fear the LORD your God for ever. (Joshua 4:21-24)

Children love to play. Even more than playing with their friends, they love to play with their parents. We are blessed to have a family fun center near us. Though we don't go often, we have several fond memories made there. The many races we have had on the go-cart track. Oh yes, this grandma is in the race too! I'm the one bumping and pushing through, pinning the unskilled grandchildren to the wall so I can pull ahead. My ever-so-aggressive son is trying to push past this road hog who thinks herself a road warrior. Then there's the bumper boats. Oh yeah! It is important to teach these little up-and-coming Mariners the skills of drowning daddy with the water cannon located on the front of the boat. It makes my heart proud to hear daddy fighting for all its worth to get away from two little girls who have mastered the art of pinning him in a corner of the pool and blasting him. One straight shooting him in the face while the other is just behind her pelting him with a high velocity arch above her sister that lands on the top of his head. I wish I had my camera on!

These memories, few though they may be, last a lifetime. They bond us together like a cord that cannot be broken. They are important. The Bible talks of memories that should never be forgotten, even after the ones who experienced them have passed on. They set stones of remembrance and tell the stories of the event. One day, their grandchildren's grandchildren will be telling the history of the pillar of stones set before them. It is important that we never forget the awesome ways that God shows up in our lives. Our children need to recognize Him in their lives as well. Who is better at teaching them than the ones who love them best? Share these important truths with your children as well.

Takeaway: It is important to teach our children how God cares for them. Show them how you learned to turn to Him by faith so they can trust Him for themselves.

Reflection Day

There are so many little ways that God communicates His love for us. He reaches out in the hugs and kisses of a child, a cup of coffee with a friend, a day at the park with family, in a simple tune on the radio, and so many more ways. What are some seemingly insignificant ways that God has reached out to you in this past week? Please take a moment to recall moments where you felt His presence and love. These will be good to reflect on later when you need a little encouragement. Just like every time we drive by the family fun center and the children begin to squeal, you will have a fond memory. A stone of remembrance to ponder on.

The Lord's Day

Dear Lord, as we close this book, I pray that you have used me to reach the heart of this person who has taken their time to read it. I pray they were able to see you a little bit better in their own life. You are always there; we just don't recognize you at times. I pray that you are more visible and real to this dear reader. I also pray that you will help this precious person to show others how to find you. Thank you, Precious Heavenly Father, for all you do and will do for us. Amen

Acknowledgements

The Lord has been so good to me over the years. He has blessed me beyond measure and given me a special gift of seeing his handiwork in such silly things as a bag of candy. I love to share these moments with others. Many of my friends and family members have encouraged me to write a book of these insights, and I want to thank them. It is my sincerest prayer that this little book is a blessing and a tool to help you see God in your own life events. God is always there. Remember that on the difficult days and remember that He truly loves you.

Special Thanks to Gwen Oldenettel and Evelyn Haxton for your continued encouragement and prayers.

Thank you to my talented daughter, Nikki, for the graphics and much more.

Made in the USA
Thornton, CO
10/15/24 14:23:17

0ae596e5-e35d-4c1a-a709-1a12e3eca1bbR01